LaRosa®

INTERNATIONAL

PASTA COOKBOOK

By Joan Nathan

Dorison House Publishers, Inc. Cambridge/New York

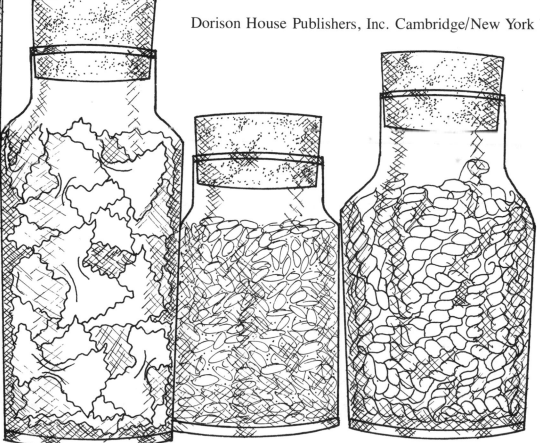

Acknowledgments

This Pasta book could never have been written without the assistance of many people. Thomas D. Torre, Vice President of V. La Rosa and Sons provided me with the necessary information about pasta and La Rosa family history. In addition, advice and information were readily available from the National Macaroni Institute, Anthony Spinazzola, Restaurant Critic of *The Boston Globe,* and my husband Allan Gerson who patiently went over every word of this manuscript.

Joan Nathan Gerson, ethnic food columnist for the Boston Globe's Sunday Magazine has lived in Italy and Israel and has worked for the United Nations, two New York mayors and the mayor of Jerusalem. She is the co-author of *The Flavor of Jerusalem,* a book about cooking and other flavorful matters in the holy city.

Copyright © 1977 by Dorison House Publishers, Inc.
Published by Dorison House Publishers, Inc.
183 Madison Avenue, New York, N.Y. 10016
ISBN: 0-916752-25-9
Library of Congress Catalog Card Number: 77-12259
Manufactured in the United States of America

Cover photo: Kenton S. Sharp
Illustration: Jerie Benson
Book Design: Cachalot Design Group
                Marblehead, Massachusetts

CONTENTS

The La Rosa Story

Ever since 1914 when Vincenzo La Rosa started the V. La Rosa and Sons Macaroni Company, La Rosa has been synonymous with succulent spaghetti, macaroni and egg noodle products flavored with pungent tomato sauces and topped with freshly grated Parmesan cheese.

It all began when Vincenzo La Rosa immigrated to the United States from Sicily. With his five sons he opened a butcher shop in the Williamsburg section of Brooklyn. During World War I, with the curtailment of foreign imports, two of his sons noticed an increased demand for spaghetti in their predominantly Italian neighborhood. One day, Stefano and Frank La Rosa suggested to their father that they start producing spaghetti in the back of the shop. What did they know about making spaghetti? Just what they had learned from watching their mother. But they learned the art of mass production very quickly. Starting with a hand press and a few pieces of elementary machinery, they set up shop in the back of their father's store.

Soon the demand for La Rosa spaghetti increased tremendously; they closed up the butcher shop and began concentrating on the products which have made their name so famous. Over 60 years and three generations later, the V. La Rosa and Sons, Inc., one of the oldest names in macaroni production nationally, manufactures over 43 varieties of spaghetti, macaroni and egg noodle products. Their main plant is located in Warminster, Pennsylvania, near Philadelphia with another plant in Milwaukee.

Four La Rosa cousins head the third generation with Vincent S. as President, Vincent F. as Executive Vice President, and Senior Vice Presidents Joseph S. and Philip P. La Rosa. A young fourth generation member, Vincent J. is presently learning the family business by acting as an apprentice in every aspect of macaroni production.

The tremendous increase in demand for macaroni products since 1914 is largely due to the mechanization of production which has enabled millions of Americans to know about ethnic products from all over the world. In 1964 La Rosa introduced the most modern automatic continuous presses and dryers into their plant facilities replacing existing equipment.

The Pasta Process

La Rosa Macaroni Products are made from hard and amber-colored durum wheat grown in North and South Dakota and parts of Montana and Minnesota. The golden wheat is then milled into semolina which is the "heart" of the durum wheat. La Rosa uses No. 1 semolina, the pure golden middlings of durum wheat to make its high quality products. The semolina is then enriched with significant amounts of vitamin B with thiamine, riboflavin, niacin and iron, all in accordance with United States government standards. Now the semolina is ready for the macaroni manufacturer.

After milling, the No. 1 semolina is tested for moisture, content and enrichment. Despite their assurance that this is the top quality available for macaroni products, the La Rosa Quality Control Laboratory tests the product in its various stages during production. Mr. Joseph S. La Rosa and the Director of Quality Control for the company visit their Midwest wheat fields and mills on a regular basis to inspect the current crops of durum wheat. Semolina samples are constantly being analyzed by La Rosa Laboratories. From purchasing of the wheat through production and packaging, at least one member of the La Rosa family has direct contact with the product.

From the mill the semolina is shipped to La Rosa's plants where it is stored in huge silos and then moved by air ducts through a sifter containing ten stages of fine screen-meshing. From the sifter the semolina passes into the macaroni press. It first enters the vacuum mixing chamber where automatic measuring devices feed the required amounts of semolina and water. Here the vacuum reduces the oxidation process during the mixing and yields a product with a higher degree of translucency owing to elimination of air bubbles in the dough. The higher the vacuum, the more golden the color of the finished product. After a mechanically timed kneading period, the dough is tested for proper consistency — a far cry from the manual labor done at the early beginning of macaroni production!

From the mixers the dough passes to a pressure chamber where under tremendous pressure (from 1500 to 2000 pounds per square inch) the dough is forced through a large bronze die containing hundreds of small holes. It is the type, size and shape of the hole which forms the spaghetti or macaroni. It is at this point that the hole is made in macaroni! More specifically, an individual die of a ziti or rigatoni, etc., has in its center a small, solid "pin" which is supported by three very thin brackets. As the dough is squeezed through the die, it passes the thin support brackets and because of the tremendous pressure it reforms again; the "pin" is large enough to prevent reformation however. Thus, the dough emerges from the die as a long tube. The size of the hole, therefore, depends upon the size of the center "pin."

After the macaroni is extruded it is then dried, a process essential to the manufacture of mass produced pasta. Drying must be accomplished from the center out in order to prevent cracking and to produce macaroni which will cook evenly. The process takes approximately 24 hours. The temperature and humidity of each dryer is scientifically controlled so that the macaroni is "cured" evenly. It is dried for a limited amount of time and then some moisture is added. (This process is repeated a number of times.) Each time less moisture remains until optimal product is achieved. The macaroni manufacturer must always keep a close watch on weather conditions so that he can accurately control all stages of the drying operation.

Once dried, the macaroni passes to packaging machines where it is weighed and boxed, glued, sealed and sent to the factory humidity-controlled warehouse rooms until shipped to the wholesaler, supermarket or neighborhood retail store.

Pasta is a generic term for spaghetti, macaroni and egg noodles and is often confusing. Spaghetti is a general term for the solid rod form of macaroni, made from semolina, vitamins and water. La Rosa's thinnest spaghetti product is Fideos and its thickest is Spaghetti. Linguine is in the shape of oval rods. Lasagne, which is also extruded in a solid shape is in a separate category.

Macaroni products other than spaghetti are the round tubular pasta products. Ziti, Elbows, Mezzani, Occhio di Lupo, and Rigatoni are examples. Partial tubes are also familiar to all of us in various sizes of shell macaroni. Egg noodles are flat, ribbon shapes or folded products made with eggs, durum flour and water. Fettuccine and egg bows are of this group.

If indeed bread is the staff of life in so many cultures, then macaroni is, at least in the western world, a close second. Combined as it usually is with proteins like meat, fish, poultry, eggs and cheese, pasta is an excellent main course. This low fat, low sodium food gives us energy from its carbohydrate content. It has more proteins than potatoes.

The La Rosa family likes to think of the United States as a country of many pots rather than a melting pot. Although pasta has the reputation of being primarily Italian, it is also Chinese with ''lo mein,'' Hungarian with ''spaetzele,'' German with ''knodel'' and Spanish with ''fideos.'' The La Rosa family would like to share with you in this book almost 200 delicious and nutritious recipes for macaroni, spaghetti and egg noodles from around the world. In some instances we will use easy and more complicated versions of the same recipe for your convenience. In addition, as a special treat, we will also include many La Rosa family Italian recipes until now savored only by members of the family and close friends.

The History of Pasta

Macaroni, spaghetti or lasagne must have originated in Italy. So most of us think. For what, after all, could be more Italian! Be however, prepared for a shock. Recently a petrified prehistoric noodle dumpling was discovered in China leading to the belief that the Chinese were eating forms of macaroni before even the Ostrogoths or the Etruscans were living in ancient Italy.

Marco Polo is credited with introducing macaroni to Italy in the 1270's after his long voyage from China. Hundreds of years before Marco Polo the Chinese had developed their own noodles. This dried wheat product, a change from pancakes, rice and breads, could be eaten hot and kept its flavor and texture better than many grain products when dried.

In the early thirteenth century, fifty years before Marco Polo's journey to the East, the Indians were eating a threadlike noodle called "sevika," the Arabs a similar one called "rishta" (also meaning thread) and the Jews of Spain "fidellos" meaning angel's hair. Pasta was probably introduced to the seaports of Italy from China via the Middle East as early as the eleventh century and even possibly centuries earlier if the Etruscans did indeed eat noodles.

Moreover, in the thirteenth and fourteenth centuries rich Italian households often included Mongul slaves who introduced Chinese noodle dishes to grace their masters' tables. At that time the most common name for pasta was "macaroni" although now this refers to tubular rather than flat types.

By the eighteenth century and the days of pilgrimages to Italy, macaroni was firmly established in European mythology. Young tourists, enamored of the many forms of macaroni, became known as "macaronis." At about the same time in England just prior to the American Revolution the term "macaroni" was a synonym for "perfection" or "elegance." The most popular slang expression of the day was "That's Macaroni," meaning "That's great." Hence the well known verse: Yankee Doodle went to town riding on a pony, stuck a feather in his hat and called it "Macaroni."

Pasta was introduced to the United States in many forms by different immigrant groups. The Germans had egg noodles, the Chinese lo mein and the Italians pasta. As early as 1802 Thomas Jefferson served a "macaroni" pie.

Many Italians who came here during the Gold Rush of 1849 were restaurant proprietors and cooks. Their simple spaghetti with tomato sauce caught on rapidly. Between the end of the nineteenth century and the beginning of World War II spaghetti had become a great American dish. With Italian sections of cities like New York, Philadelphia, Boston, Chicago and San Francisco, located next to melting pots of many ethnic backgrounds, non-Italians started to taste the exotic inexpensive fare of their Italian neighbors. At first pasta could only be bought from select gourmet grocers whose shops were filled with imported pastas, cheese and sauces.

Two major events increased pasta production in this country. When World War I cut off imports from abroad, local production like that of V. La Rosa & Sons, Inc. was essential. Secondly, pressure from the ever growing group of domestic pasta manufacturers, forced the Department of Agriculture to encourage farmers in the Midwest to grow the durum wheat which has the hard quality needed for good firm pasta dough. At about the same time, food companies learned to can tomatoes and tomato sauces. Soon products like prepared sauces and raviolis were available to the consumer. Spaghetti products have become such a staple American food that, according to the National Macaroni Manufacturer's Association there are today over 150 varieties of macaroni available in the United States. In the United States, at the present time, the per capita consumption is approximately 8 pounds per person, with the greatest consumption taking place in the East.

The Legends of Macaroni

As in so many foods the origin of macaroni is veiled in legend. Was it China or Italy that gave birth to this loved product? We have no way of knowing wherein lies the truth. The following are several of the most popular macaroni legends:

THE LEGEND OF THE LEAF (or the Origin of Chinese Noodles)
One fine spring day hundreds of years before the beginning of the Christian era, a gust of wind caused a leaf to flutter into the bread dough a Chinese woman was preparing for baking. Before she realized that it had happened, the leaf became deeply imbedded in the dough. Pondering how she might remove the leaf without wasting precious dough, the cook looked about for an answer. Reaching for her sieve, she forced the dough through it, using a big wooden spoon. The dough, of course, came through in strands. Then a strange idea occurred to her. "Why not dry the narrow strands in the sun, instead of baking them?" Thus, because of a falling leaf, a delightful new food was discovered. Yes, that is how we came to have Macaroni. So says the legend.

A LEGEND OF LOVE (or How Macaroni was first Discovered)
One day, in about the year 1270, a young Chinese maiden was busy preparing her daily batch of bread dough. Becoming engrossed in conversation with an ardent Italian sailor who happened to be a member of the great explorer, Marco Polo's crew, she forgot her task. Soon the dough overflowed from the pan and dripped onto a nearby rock in strings that quickly dried in the sun. When he observed what had happened, the young Italian, hoping to hide the evidence of his loved one's carelessness, gathered the strings of dried dough and took them to his ship. The ship's inventive cook boiled them in a broth. He was pleased to find that the result was an appetizing and savory dish. Tradition has it that the great Marco Polo himself, enjoyed if not this first dish of pasta, then the chef's second or third attempt at creating this early form of pasta. Upon the ship's return to Italy, word of the delicious new dish spread rapidly, and soon it was popular throughout the land. Thus, says this legend, was macaroni discovered.

THE LEGEND OF AN EPICURE (or The Origin of the Word "Macaroni")
A thirteenth century wealthy nobleman of Palermo who was noted for his love of fine food, possessed a cook with a marvelous inventive genius. One day this talented cook devised the farinaceous tubes with which we are familiar today . . . and served them with rich sauce and grated parmesan cheese in a large china bowl. The first mouthful caused the illustrious epicure to shout, "Cari!", or in idiomatic English, "The darlings!" With the second mouthful, he emphasized his statement, exclaiming, "Ma Cari!, Ah, but what darlings!" And as the flavor of the dish grew upon him his enthusiasm rose to even greater heights, "Ah, 'Ma Caroni', but dearest darlings!" In paying this supreme tribute to his cook's discovery, the nobleman bestowed the name by which this admirable preparation is known today . . . Macaroni!

10

THE LEGEND OF THE DOUGH MEN (or Still Another Origin of Macaroni)

During the thirteenth century, bakers in Germany made a practice of fashioning dough into large symbolic figures. These they baked and served as bread. The unique figures resembled men, stars, swords, birds, seashells and the like. Called dough men by their originators, these food products presently were brought by German merchants to Genoa, Italy. At first, the Genoese were reluctant to buy them because of their large form and high price. To the merchants they protested ''Ma Caroni,'' which today Italian dictionaries give as meaning ''But it is very dear.'' Thus, in order to obtain new trade, the Germans found it wise to reduce the size of the dough forms and to reduce the prices proportionately. Yet strangely enough, the name given to these unusual figures never changed. The smaller dough men were still called Macaroni.

Manner of Basic Cooking

Second to the production of high quality pasta is the cooking of it. For many people, myself included, pasta is one staple food difficult to judge portion-wise and then tricky to insure that it is *"al dente"* or firm but tender to the tooth — not soggy!

Quantity to Cook:

Generally speaking it is safe to say that 2 ounces of uncooked pasta per person can be allowed in a main dish. *However,* make sure you know the appetites of your family and guests beforehand. For many, 4 ounces of spaghetti is the logical amount for one serving.

The following table will be helpful in indicating the amount of pasta to cook when one type is substituted for another and in deciding how much will be needed for any given number of persons. It may be helpful to know that macaroni and spaghetti are approximately double in volume after cooking, while egg noodles remain about the same.

Product	Dry	Cooked
Elbow Macaroni	8 ounces	4½ cups (approx.)
Spaghetti	8 ounces	5 cups (approx.)
Egg Noodles	8 ounces	4 cups (approx.)

How to Cook

Allowing *2 ounces* pasta per person, let us cook *8 ounces* for *4 people*. Remember when larger amounts of pasta are used allow *4 to 6 quarts of water* and *2 tablespoons salt* for *each pound of macaroni, spaghetti or noodles*.

1. Heat *3 quarts* of water in a large saucepot to a rapid boil.
2. Gradually add *8 ounces* of spaghetti, egg noodles (4 cups) or macaroni and *1 tablespoon salt*. Spaghetti is the trickiest. Grasp one handful and place one end of the strands fanned out in the water; as it softens gently swoosh the pasta into the water, until it is all submerged. Be sure the water continues to boil. The rapid and continuous boiling helps to keep the macaroni moving about so it will cook quickly and evenly.
3. Cook, *uncovered,* stirring occasionally and gently, until tender. Again, for the spaghetti a wooden spaghetti fork is especially helpful at separating the strands so that they will cook evenly and not stick together. Stirring insures that all the pasta will be cooked at the same time.
4. The pasta is done when it is "al dente." Taste a piece of pasta for doneness. Cooking time will vary with the size and thickness of macaroni product being used. Small pasta might take 2 minutes while large thick macaroni might take 15. The average time is from *8 to 10 minutes*. Check the package directions for exact time. If the macaroni is to be used in a casserole and receive further cooking, cook a shorter time.
5. *Drain the pasta immediately in a colander.* Serve as rapidly as possible, or mix with other ingredients in the recipe. *Rinse only if* the macaroni is to be used in a cold salad. Then, rinse with cold water and drain again.
6. Eat with gusto and enjoy!

Glossary of Pasta Terms

Note: All the following terms are from the Italian unless otherwise indicated.

A La Casalinga — homestyle

Acini di Pepe — tiny square or rounds of pasta used in soup.

Aglio e Olio — garlic and oil

Agnolotti, agnelotti — ravioli squares of pasta filled with various savory stuffings. They are served dry with butter and grated cheese or smothered in meat gravy.

Al Burro — with butter

Al dente — "to the tooth" — cooked medium-firm, consistency in which pasta tastes best

Bucatini — "small cave or hole", long macaroni with small hole

Budino di Pasta — noodle pudding

Cacciatora — "hunter" style — with wine, garlic, subtle herbs and usually onions, olives and tomatoes

Cannelloni — "big pipes" — large tubes of pasta filled with cheese, minced meat or fish and served in a rich tomato and cheese sauce

Capelli d'Angelo — "angel's hair" — a very thin pasta

Capellini — hair-thin noodles

Carbonara — a process named after old-time charcoal gatherers who went into the woods laden for a stay with spaghetti, smoked ham, olive oil, hard cheese and eggs. All these items were combined in one dish and seasoned with coarse black pepper. The results were so good that "spaghetti alla carbonara" is now served with considerable ceremony in the best restaurants.

Ditali — short tubular form of pasta shaped like a thimble

Ditalini — small thimble shaped pasta

Fettuccine — flat, ribbon-shaped egg pasta

    al burro — with butter

    Alfredo — with cheese, cream, and eggs — originally prepared in Rome

Fideos — (Spanish) extra thin spaghetti

Fiorentina — alla — Florentine style; usually has spinach in it

Fusilli — long strips of spiral pasta

Imbottitto — stuffed, baked

Knodel — (German), noodles

14

Lasagne — 2 inch wide pasta prepared in different ways in different places, usually used layered with vegetables, meat and cheese or sometimes rolled with a filling and covered with sauce before baking

Lokshen — (Yiddish), noodle

Maccheroni — any form of macaroni, noodles or spaghetti

Mafalde — twisted noodles

Manicotti — ''muffs'' — large, hollow tubes of pasta for stuffing with a variety of ingredients such as meat and cheese, and baked in a sauce

Marinara, alla — ''sailor style'', in a spicy meatless sauce

Maruzze — large shells from Naples

Maruzzelle — medium shells from Naples

Maruzzini — small shells from Naples

Mezzani — smaller plain tubular, shortcut macaroni from Naples

Minestrone — thick, vegetable soup

Mostaccioli — angular cut tubular macaroni — served with salmon, tuna or other fish and prepared in a casserole

Mostaccioli Rigati — angular cut ribbed tubular macaroni

Nouilles — (French), noodles

Occhio du Lupo — ''eyes of the wolf'', very large Napolitani, smooth macaroni similar to Rigatoni

Orzo — barley, used in soup

Pasta — generic term for all kinds of noodles, macaroni, spaghetti, etc. All pasta has a wheat-flour base, but comes in an incredible variety of shapes and sizes

Pasta e Fagioli — pasta and beans

Pastina — very small egg product for babies and soup

Perciatelli — long, tubular macaroni

Pesto — Famous Genoese sauce to enliven lasagne, gnocchi, minestrone or linguine. Ingredients are garlic, oil, basil, Sardinia sheep's milk cheese or parmesan and pine nuts.

Pignoli — pine nuts

Pot au Feu — (French), traditional beef vegetable soup with pasta

Ragu — a popular sauce consisting of olive oil, butter, meat and garlic

Ravioli — moist cheese or meat stuffed pasta

Ricotta — a fresh creamed cheese with a mild flavor, resembling cottage cheese

Rigatoni — large ribbed tubular macaroni

Ripieno — stuffing, filling

Spaghetti — general term for solid rod form of macaroni. Round rods are made in many different diameters, used with sauce, meatballs and cheese

    all'amatriciani — with bacon, onion, fresh tomato sauce

    alla bolognese — in tomato and thick meat sauce

    alla carbonara — tossed with raw egg, grated parmesan and romano cheese, bits of ham or salt pork

alla chitarra — very thin

alla sua cusana — with eggplant, anchovies and olives

alle vongole — with clams and tomato sauce

con carne — with meat

Spaghettini — thin form of spaghetti used with sauce, meatballs and cheese

Spatzele — (Hungarian), tiny dumplings

Stracotto — extra cooked, like pot roast

Tagliatelle — flat, narrow noodles

verde — colored green with spinach juice

Tetrazzini — an American chicken, cheese and spaghetti dish named after an opera singer who was crazy about pasta

Trenette — thin, long noodles

Tubetti — small short cut tubular macaroni

Tubettini — smaller tubular short cut macaroni

Umido — in stew

Tufoli — similar to Cannelloni, only smaller

Vermicelli — wispy-thin spaghetti

Ziti — plain short cut macaroni

HORS D'OEUVRES
AND SALADS

Pasta for Party Pick-ups? Why not! The following stuffed shell macaroni finger fare may be served with your favorite drink before dinner. Serve macaroni salad, shrimp or crabmeat with pasta as an elegant first course, or consider pasta salad for your luncheon or picnic main dish. Macaroni salad is always a welcome side dish which combines deliciously with meat or fish all year round.

BLEU CHEESE SPREAD

2 ounces bleu cheese
1 tablespoon evaporated milk or cream
Dash of Worcestershire sauce

¼ teaspoon paprika
24 cooked large shells

1. Crumble cheese.
2. Add milk, Worcestershire sauce and paprika. Mix thoroughly. Stuff shells.
Makes 24 hors d'oeuvres.

PORK SAUSAGE

½ pound medium sized pork sausages
36 cooked large shells
4 gherkins

1. Put sausages in frying pan with 3 tablespoons water. Cover closely and steam for 5 minutes. Remove cover and sauté until dry. Cut each sausage into 9 slices. Put one slice of sausage cut down, into each shell. Garnish with thin slice of gherkin.
Makes 36 hors d'oeuvres.

EGG SPREAD

1 hard-boiled egg
¼ cup finely diced pickle
1 teaspoon lemon juice
1 tablespoon mayonnaise

¼ teaspoon salt
Dash of pepper
36 cooked large shells
Paprika

1. Mince the egg. Add the remaining ingredients except the paprika and shells.
2. Fill shells and sprinkle lightly with paprika.
Makes 36 hors d'oeuvres.

LIVERWURST SPREAD

¼ pound liverwurst
2 tablespoons mayonnaise

48 cooked large shells
1 pimiento

1. Peel casing off liverwurst. Add mayonnaise, mixing thoroughly.
2. Fill shells. Garnish with tiny strip of pimiento.
Makes 48 hors d'oeuvres.

SHRIMP PASTE

1 cup cooked shrimp
1 tablespoon lemon juice
1 tablespoon ketchup

1 tablespoon mayonnaise
48 cooked large shells

1. Mince shrimp. Add lemon juice, ketchup and mayonnaise. Mix thoroughly.
2. Stuff shells.
Makes 48 hors d'oeuvres.

PICNIC BEAN SALAD

1 package Ditalini
3 tablespoons Italian-style salad dressing
3 tablespoons mayonnaise
½ cup diced green pepper
1 cup diced celery

¼ cup Italian-style salad dressing
1 (15½ ounce) can kidney beans or
  chick peas
Salad greens

1. Cook Ditalini according to directions on package; drain. Rinse in cold water; drain again.
2. Toss Ditalini with 3 tablespoons Italian-style salad dressing and chill, at least one hour.
3. Combine mayonnaise with green pepper, celery, ¼ cup more Italian-style salad dressing and add to chilled macaroni; toss well. Gently fold in kidney beans or chick peas which have been drained. Serve on salad greens.
Serves 6–8.

CARNIVAL SALAD

1 package Ditalini
½ cup Italian-style salad dressing
1 cup diced celery
1 cup diced green pepper
½ cup coarsely chopped sweet pickles
¼ cup grated onion

2 small cans sliced mushrooms
Salad greens
Cucumber wheels for garnish
Sliced stuffed olives for garnish
Strips of pimientos for garnish

1. Cook the Ditalini according to the directions on package; drain, rinse in cold water and drain again.
2. Combine Italian-style salad dressing with celery, green pepper, sweet pickles, grated onion, & mushrooms, drained. Mix well with the macaroni, adding more salad dressing if necessary. Chill.
3. Serve on a bed of salad greens and decorate with unpared cucumber wheels, sliced stuffed olives and strips of pimientos.

Serves 6–8.

PICNIC CHICKEN MACARONI SALAD

4 ounces elbow macaroni
2 cups diced cooked chicken
1 cup chopped apples
1 cup diced celery
¾ cup chopped walnuts
½ cup diced sweet pickle
2 tablespoons chopped onion

½ cup mayonnaise
1 tablespoon prepared mustard
2 tablespoons lemon juice
1 teaspoon salt
Dash of pepper
Endive, watercress or lettuce
Pimiento strips

1. Cook elbows according to directions on package. Drain, rinse with cold water and drain again.
2. While elbows are cooking, combine chicken, apples, celery, nuts, pickles and onion. Mix mayonnaise, mustard, lemon juice, salt and pepper. Combine chicken mixture, elbows and salad dressing. Chill well. Serve on curly endive, watercress, or lettuce. Garnish with pimiento strips.

Serves 4.

SAVORY MACARONI AND EGG SALAD

½ pound Ditali macaroni
4 stalks celery, diced
1 small onion, chopped
3 hard-boiled eggs, cut up

½ cup Italian style salad dressing
¼ cup mayonnaise
Salad greens
Paprika

1. Cook Ditali following package directions. Drain, rinse in cold water and drain again.
2. Mix the celery, onion, eggs, salad dressing and mayonnaise and fold into the macaroni, tossing and mixing well. Chill. Serve on bed of salad greens. Sprinkle lightly with paprika.

Serves 4–6.

COTTAGE CHEESE SALAD

2 cups shell macaroni
¼ cup French dressing
2 cups cottage cheese
4 tablespoons diced pimiento
¼ cup diced green pepper
¼ cup chopped chives

¼ cup diced radish
1 cup sour cream
2 tablespoons lemon juice
½ teaspoon salt
½ teaspoon dry powdered mustard
Salad greens

1. Cook shells according to directions on package. Drain, rinse with cold water and drain again.
2. Add the French dressing, cottage cheese, pimiento, green pepper, chives and radish.
3. Make a dressing by blending the sour cream, lemon juice, salt and mustard in a blender or food processor. Add to salad and mix thoroughly. Serve on salad greens.

Serves 4.

22

EASTER EGG SALAD

6 ounces elbow macaroni
½ cup mayonnaise
2 tablespoons French dressing
1 teaspoon salt
3 drops Tabasco sauce (optional)

1 cup cooked kidney beans
3 diced hard boiled eggs
¼ cup chopped sweet or sour pickles
Watercress

1. Cook elbow macaroni according to directions on package. Drain, rinse and drain again.
2. While macaroni is cooking, combine mayonnaise, French dressing, salt and Tabasco sauce. Fold in kidney beans, eggs, pickles and macaroni. Chill well. Serve on nests of watercress.

Serves 4.

JULIENNE SALAD

⅓ package elbow macaroni
½ cup mayonnaise
1 teaspoon prepared mustard
2 tablespoons chili sauce
12 ounces sliced ham and turkey in
   julienne strips

1 teaspoon salt
3 diced hard boiled eggs
1 cup cooked peas
Lettuce leaves

1. Cook macaroni according to directions on package; drain.
2. While macaroni is cooking, combine mayonnaise, mustard, chili sauce and salt.
3. Add julienne of ham and turkey, eggs, peas and macaroni. Chill well. Serve on lettuce leaves.

Serves 4.

FRUIT SALAD

2 cups elbow macaroni
½ cup French dressing
1 cup diced celery
2 cups unpeeled diced apples
1 cup chopped seedless raisins

6 chopped walnuts
1 peeled diced orange
1 cup mayonnaise or ½ cup mayonnaise
   and ½ cup heavy whipped cream
Salad greens

1. Cook elbow macaroni according to directions on package. Rinse with cold water and drain well.
2. Add French dressing, celery, apples, raisins, walnuts, orange and mayonnaise and mix thoroughly. Serve garnished with salad greens.

Serves 4–6

FRENCH MACARONI SALAD

2 cups elbow macaroni
½ cup French dressing
1 cup finely diced celery
¼ cup finely sliced scallions
   including tops

2 tablespoons chopped parsley
¾ cup mayonnaise
2 tablespoons prepared mustard
1½ tablespoons lemon juice
Salad greens

1. Cook elbow macaroni according to directions on package. Rinse with cold water and drain well.
2. Add French dressing, celery, scallions and parsley. Combine the mayonnaise, mustard and lemon juice. Add to salad. Mix thoroughly. Serve garnished with salad greens.

Serves 6.

PEANUT AND CABBAGE SALAD

2 cups shell macaroni
¼ cup French dressing
2 cups shredded cabbage
¾ cup chopped unsalted peanuts

½ cup mayonnaise
3 tablespoons cream or evaporated milk
Salad greens

1. Cook shells according to directions on package. Drain and rinse with cold water. Drain again.
2. Add French dressing, cabbage and peanuts. Combine mayonnaise and cream. Add to salad. Mix thoroughly. Serve garnished with salad greens.

Serves 6.

HAM MOUSSE FILLED WITH MACARONI

1 package unflavored gelatine
1¼ cups hot water
2 cups ground cooked ham
1 teaspoon dry or prepared mustard
Dash cayenne pepper
2 tablespoons grated onion
2 tablespoons diced green pepper
2 tablespoons chopped parsley
2 tablespoons lemon juice

½ cup heavy cream (whipped)
2 cups shell macaroni
¼ cup French dressing
1 cup diced cucumber
½ cup diced radish
¼ cup chopped parsley
½ pimiento, sliced
½ cup mayonnaise
Salad greens

1. Dissolve gelatine in hot water, adding ham, mustard, cayenne pepper, onion, green pepper, parsley and lemon juice. Cool. Fold in whipped cream. Turn into one quart ring mold. Chill until firm.
2. Cook shells according to directions on package. Rinse with cold water and drain well.
3. Add the French dressing, cucumber, radish, parsley, pimiento and mayonnaise. Mix thoroughly.
4. Turn ring mold out onto serving dish. Fill center with macaroni mixture. Garnish with salad greens.

Serves 4–6.

ONION AND ORANGE SALAD

3 cups shell macaroni
½ cup French dressing
1 cup diced Bermuda onion

3 diced navel oranges
1 cup mayonnaise
Salad greens

1. Cook shells according to directions on package. Rinse with cold water and drain.
2. Add French dressing, onion, oranges and mayonnaise. Mix thoroughly. Serve garnished with salad greens.

Serves 4–6.

SHRIMP 'N' SHELL SALAD WITH HERB DRESSING

½ pound medium shells
1 pound cooked shrimp, coarsely chopped
1 package (9 ounces) frozen cut
   green beans, cooked and drained
1 red onion, cut into thin rings
2 tablespoons chopped pimiento

3 tablespoons oil
¼ cup lemon juice
1 clove minced garlic
1 teaspoon salt
½ teaspoon thyme
¼ teaspoon oregano

1. Cook shells according to directions on package; drain and rinse in cold water; drain again.
2. Mix shells in a bowl with shrimp, green beans, onion and pimiento.
3. Combine oil with lemon juice, garlic, salt, thyme and oregano, blending well. Pour over macaroni mixture; mix to coat all ingredients well. Cover and refrigerate for 1 hour.

Serves 4–6.

TUNA, MUSHROOM AND MACARONI SALAD

½ pound fresh mushrooms, thinly sliced
2 teaspoons lemon juice
¼ cup thinly sliced scallions
3 tablespoons olive oil
½ teaspoon salt

¼ teaspoon thyme
8 ounces elbow macaroni
1 (7-ounce) can tuna chunks
8–10 black olives, sliced

1. In a wooden or glass bowl, toss the mushrooms with the lemon juice until the slices are lightly moistened. Then add scallions, oil, salt, and thyme and toss again.
2. Cook macaroni as directed on package; drain, rinse and drain again.
3. Add macaroni, tuna and olives and set aside to chill until serving.
Serves 4.

TOMATO ASPIC WITH CRABMEAT

3½ cups tomato juice
2 packages unflavored gelatine
1 teaspoon salt
Dash of pepper
2 tablespoons lemon juice
1½ cups shell macaroni
¼ cup French dressing

1 cup diced celery
1 cup diced cooked fresh or
   canned crab meat
1 peeled diced tomato
¼ cup diced green pepper
½ cup mayonnaise
Salad greens

1. Heat ½ the tomato juice. Dissolve the unflavored gelatine in it. Add rest of tomato juice, salt and pepper and lemon juice. Pour into 1 quart ring mold and chill until firm.
2. Cook shells according to directions on package. Drain, rinse with cold water and drain again.
3. Add French dressing, celery, crab meat, tomato, green pepper and mayonnaise, mixing thoroughly. Turn aspic mold onto serving dish. Fill center with macaroni mixture. Serve garnished with salad greens.
Serves 4–6.

SHRIMP AND PINEAPPLE SALAD

2 cups elbow macaroni
¼ cup French dressing
1½ cups cooked shrimp
1½ cups diced pineapple

¼ cup diced pimiento
½ cup mayonnaise
8 stuffed olives
Salad greens

1. Cook elbow macaroni according to directions on package. Drain and rinse with cold water and drain again.
2. Add French dressing, shrimp, pineapple, pimiento and mayonnaise. Mix thoroughly. Serve on platter garnished with stuffed olives and salad greens.

Serves 4.

TOMATO SURPRISE SALAD

4 medium tomatoes
1 cup Tubettini (small tubular macaroni)
¼ cup French dressing
1 cup diced celery

1 cup diced cooked chicken
½ cup mayonnaise
Salad greens

1. Slice off top of the tomatoes, and scoop out center to form a hollow cup. Reserve ½ cup diced tomato pulp.
2. Cook Tubettini according to directions on package. Drain, rinse with cold water and drain again.
3. Add tomato pulp, French dressing, diced celery, chicken and mayonnaise. Mix thoroughly. Stuff tomatoes with mixture. Serve garnished with salad greens.

Serves 4.

MACARONI TUNA SALAD

½ pound elbow macaroni
1 small green pepper, diced
1 small onion, chopped
1 cup sliced celery
1 large can (13 ounces) flaked tuna fish

¾ cup sliced mustard pickles
½ cup sour cream
Salt and pepper to taste
Salad greens

1. Cook elbow macaroni according to directions on package. Drain, rinse and drain again.
2. Combine green pepper, onion, celery, tuna, pickles, sour cream, salt and pepper and fold into macaroni, mixing well. Chill. Serve on salad greens.

Serves 4–6.

MACARONI VEGETABLE SALAD

2 cups elbow macaroni
10 ounces frozen peas
5 medium carrots, cut into pieces
1 medium unpeeled cucumber, scored
  and thinly sliced
10 large radishes, thinly sliced
½ cup sliced celery
¼ cup finely chopped parsley

¾ cup salad oil
¼ cup lemon juice
3 tablespoons prepared mustard
2 tablespoons finely chopped onion
1 tablespoon salt
¼ teaspoon pepper
1 medium garlic clove, crushed

1. Cook macaroni according to directions on package; drain, rinse in cold water and drain again.
2. Place frozen peas in bowl. Cover with boiling water and let stand 1 to 2 minutes; drain.
3. In a large bowl, arrange cooked macaroni, peas, carrots, cucumber, radishes, celery and parsley. Cover and chill. When ready to serve, combine salad oil, lemon juice, mustard, chopped onion, salt, pepper and clove in a covered container. Shake well. Toss lightly with macaroni mixture.

Note: Salad may be mixed with dressing and chilled 3 hours, if desired. Toss well before serving.

Serves 6–8.

SOUPS

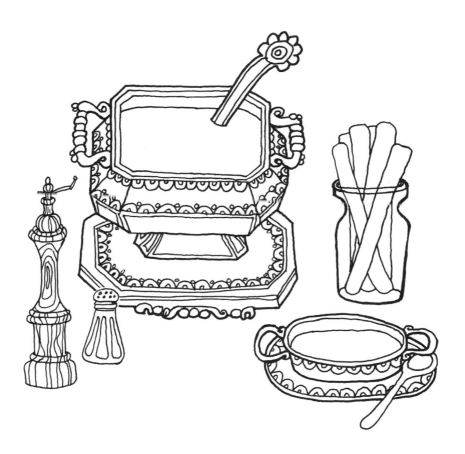

Soups are a natural perked up with pasta. Add orzo, alphabets or unusual twisted macaroni shapes to your family favorite or try the following recipes for a new luncheon or dinner dish.

RUSSIAN BORSCHT

1 cup diced onion
2 tablespoons butter or margarine
4 beets

1 quart seasoned beef broth
2 cups thinly sliced raw cabbage
1 cup Ditalini

1. Sauté onion in butter or margarine.
2. Peel beets and dice. Add beets and beef broth to onions. Cover pot and simmer 20 minutes. Then add cabbage.
3. Cook Ditalini according to directions on package. Drain and add. Serve with a dollop of sour cream. Borscht is delicious hot in winter and cold in summer.

Serves 4–6.

SPANISH STYLE CHICKEN SOUP WITH FIDEOS

1 (2 pound) chicken
2 small chopped onions
1 small green pepper
3 cloves garlic
3 coriander leaves

9½ cups water
2½ teaspoons salt
1 pound potatoes
6 ounces Fideos (hairlike spaghetti)

1. Boil chicken, onions, green pepper, garlic, coriander leaves and salt in water. When boiling, cover and simmer one hour. Strain.
2. Shred and replace chicken in the broth; add potatoes and Fideos. Cook an additional 15 minutes.

Serves 4–6.

LETTUCE AND LASAGNE SOUP

1 bunch scallions, chopped
¼ cup olive oil or vegetable oil
1 head lettuce, cut into strips
2 quarts chicken or beef broth

½ pound Lasagne
3 tablespoons butter
Salt and pepper to taste
Grated Parmesan cheese

1. Sauté chopped scallions in a large pot with the oil until scallions are transparent, around 5 minutes. Add lettuce and simmer for 5 minutes. Add broth. Heat to boil.
2. Add Lasagne, cooking for about 15 minutes uncovered. Add butter, salt and pepper. Sprinkle with Parmesan cheese.

Serves 4–6.

FRENCH CANADIAN SPLIT PEA SOUP

½ pound dried green split peas
1 bay leaf
6 cups water
2 tablespoons chopped ham
¼ cup diced onion
¼ cup diced celery

¼ cup diced carrots
3 tablespoons vegetable oil or olive oil
2 tablespoons chopped parsley
2 teaspoons salt
1 cup Tubettini (small tubular macaroni)

1. Add peas and bay leaf to water and boil in covered casserole until tender.
2. Sauté ham, onion, celery and carrots in oil. Then add to peas. Bring to boil. Add parsley and salt and stir.
3. Cook Tubettini according to directions on package; drain.
4. Combine all ingredients and serve hot.

Serves 4–6.

EASY CHICKEN NOODLE SOUP

1 quart seasoned chicken broth
½ cup diced carrots
½ cup diced chicken meat

3 ounces egg noodles
1 tablespoon chopped parsley

1. Simmer broth, carrots and chicken meat 5 minutes in covered pot.
2. Add egg noodles. Simmer 10 minutes covered. Add parsley and serve.
Serves 4–6.

EASY EGG NOODLE SOUP

1 quart seasoned beef broth
3 ounces egg noodles
¼ cup grated Parmesan cheese

1. Simmer broth in covered pot.
2. Add egg noodles and cook until tender.
3. Serve with grated cheese.
Serves 4.

ONION SOUP

1 quart seasoned beef broth
⅓ cup vegetable oil
1 quart sliced onions
Pinch of pepper

Few drops Tabasco sauce
1 cup Tubetti (tubular macaroni)
Grated Parmesan cheese

1. Simmer broth in covered pot.
2. Sauté onions lightly in oil and add.
3. Add pepper, Tabasco, and Tubetti and cook 15 minutes covered in pot.
4. Serve with grated cheese.
Serves 4–6.

EASY BOUILLON CUBE SOUP

1 quart water
4 beef or chicken bouillon cubes

Pepper to taste
½ cup Pastina

1. Heat water. Add bouillon cubes and dissolve. Add pepper and bring to boil.
2. Add Pastina. Boil 5 minutes, stirring thoroughly.
Serves 4–6.

ALPHABET CONSOMMÉ

1 quart seasoned chicken broth
½ cup diced celery

½ cup diced carrots
⅓ package alphabet macaroni

1. Heat chicken broth to boiling. Add celery and carrots. Simmer 5 minutes in covered pot.
2. Boil alphabets according to directions on package. Drain. Add to chicken stock.
Serves 4–6.

GARDEN VEGETABLE SOUP

¼ pound dried white beans
2 cups water
1 cup diced celery
¼ cup diced onions
½ cup diced carrots

¼ cup butter or margarine
1 cup finely sliced string beans
1 quart seasoned beef broth
2 cups Maruzzelle (medium shells)

1. Soak the beans in water overnight. Simmer in same water until tender.
2. Sauté celery, onions and carrots in butter or margarine. Then add to beans in water.
3. Add string beans and beef broth and simmer.
4. Cook Marruzzelle shells according to directions on package. Drain and add to soup.
Serves 4–6.

35

PASTA E FAGIOLI (Bean and Macaroni Soup)

1 medium onion, chopped
1 clove garlic, minced
1 stalk celery, chopped
3 tablespoons olive oil
½ (16 ounce) can tomatoes, drained
   and cut up

1 teaspoon salt
Pepper to taste
1 quart warm water
½ pound Ditali
1 (16 ounce) can white or red kidney beans
Grated Parmesan cheese

1. Brown the onion, garlic and celery in olive oil. Add tomatoes, salt, pepper and warm water. Bring to a boil.
2. Add Ditali, and cook for about 8 to 10 minutes or until almost tender. Then add white or red kidney beans with their liquid. Mix, cover and cook for another 5 minutes or until macaroni is tender and beans heated through. Serve with grated cheese.

Serves 4.

Note: if a thinner soup is desired, add more water.

MACARONI AND PEA SOUP

¼ cup chopped onion
1 clove garlic, minced
¼ cup chopped celery
2 tablespoons olive oil
1 quart chicken broth or water
2 tablespoons tomato paste

½ pound Ditalini
Salt and pepper to taste
1 (1 pound) can peas, drained
Grated Parmesan cheese
Diced boiled ham or frankfurters,
   optional

1. Brown onion, garlic and celery in olive oil. Add warm chicken broth or water and tomato paste; stir until tomato paste dissolves.
2. Add Ditalini and season to taste with salt and pepper; simmer 8 to 10 minutes or until the macaroni is almost tender. Then add drained peas. Mix, cover and cook for another 5 minutes, or until the macaroni is tender. Serve sprinkled with grated parmesan cheese.

Serves 4–6.

Note: If a thinner soup is desired add more water. Diced boiled ham or thin slices of frankfurter may be added.

TOMATO CORN CHOWDER

2 cups Maruzzelle (small shells)
2 strips bacon, diced
½ cup diced onions
½ cup diced celery

3½ cups tomatoes
1 cup cooked whole kernel corn
1½ teaspoon salt

1. Bring Maruzzelle to boil in 1 quart water.
2. Brown bacon and add. Sauté onions and celery in bacon fat and add. Add tomatoes, corn and salt.
3. Continue boiling until Maruzzelle shells are tender.

Serves 4–6.

FISH CHOWDER

6 cups water
1½ pounds raw cod
1 bay leaf
2 tablespoons diced onion
⅔ cup sliced carrot
1 clove finely chopped garlic
2 tablespoons vegetable oil
1 cup diced raw tomatoes

1 teaspoon curry powder
1 teaspoon grated lemon rind
2 tablespoons lemon juice
1 tablespoon salt
¼ teaspoon pepper
2 tablespoons minced parsley
1 cup Ditalini (tubular macaroni)

1. Bring water to boil in a large covered pot. Add cod and bay leaf and simmer 5 minutes covered. Remove fish. Keep fish stock. Separate fish from skin and bones, breaking fish meat into small pieces.
2. Sauté onion, carrot and garlic with fish in oil and add to fish stock. Simmer, covered, 15 minutes. Add tomatoes, curry powder, lemon rind, lemon juice, salt, pepper and parsley to stock. Cover and simmer.
3. Meanwhile, cook Ditalini according to directions on package; drain. Add to chowder and serve.

Serves 6.

POT AU FEU

6 cups water
1 pound chuck
1 small soup bone, cracked
1 bay leaf
1 cup diced carrots
¼ cup diced onion

½ cup diced celery
2 tablespoons parsley
2 teaspoons salt
Dash of pepper
3 tablespoons vegetable oil
1 cup Ditalini (tubular macaroni)

1. Bring 6 cups water to boil in a pot. Add beef, bone, and bay leaf. Simmer covered until beef is tender. Remove beef, bone and bay leaf.
2. Sauté carrots, onion, celery, parsley, salt and pepper in oil and add to meat stock. Cut beef into cubes and add.
3. Add Ditalini. Simmer 15 minutes covered.
Serves 4–6.

LENTIL MACARONI SOUP

½ cup diced salt pork
⅓ cup chopped onion
½ cup sliced celery
1 cup thinly sliced carrots
1½ quarts water
1½ cups lentils, well rinsed

1 (8-ounce) can tomatoes
2 tablespoons chopped parsley
1½ teaspoons salt
¼ teaspoon rubbed sage
Dash of pepper
½ cup elbow macaroni

1. In a large saucepan, brown salt pork. Add onion, celery and carrots and cook until the onion is lightly browned.
2. Add water, lentils, tomatoes, parsley, salt, sage, and pepper and bring to a boil. Cover tightly and simmer gently 30 minutes. Stir in macaroni and cook covered until macaroni is tender, about 10 to 15 minutes.
Serves 6–8.

QUICK MINESTRONE

¼ cup chopped onion
1 clove minced garlic
1 tablespoon butter
1 tablespoon olive oil
1 tablespoon tomato paste
2 quarts chicken or beef broth

8 ounces elbow macaroni
2 (1 pound) cans mixed garden
   vegetables with liquid
Salt and pepper to taste
Parmesan or Romano cheese

1. Sauté onion and garlic in butter and olive oil until soft and transparent. Stir in tomato paste; add broth.
2. Add macaroni, bring to a boil again and cook 10 to 12 minutes, or until tender.
3. Add vegetables for the last 5 minutes, season to taste with salt and pepper and serve with grated Parmesan or Romano cheese.

Serves 4–6.

FLORENTINE MINESTRONE*

1 quart seasoned beef stock
⅓ cup diced raw carrots
1 clove finely minced garlic
⅓ cup sliced onion
¼ cup chopped cooked ham
1 tablespoon vegetable oil
1 cup cauliflower

1 cup diced zucchini
⅓ cup diced celery
1 cup cooked red kidney beans
2 cups chopped spinach
1 tablespoon chopped parsley
2 cups Ditalini
Grated Parmesan cheese

1. Combine the beef stock and the carrots. Simmer 10 minutes.
2. Sauté the garlic, onion and ham in oil and add to soup.
3. Add the cauliflower, zucchini, celery, kidney beans and spinach and cook 10 minutes more. Then add the parsley.
4. Cook the Ditalini according to directions on package; drain and add. Serve with grated cheese.

Serves 4–6.

*Florentine style usually has spinach in it.

CHICKEN AND VEGETABLE POTAGE WITH PASTINA

One 3 pound frying chicken
¼ cup butter or margarine
2 quarts boiling water
1 tablespoon salt
Dash white pepper

1 cup carrots sliced in julienne strips
1 cup celery cut in julienne strips
½ cup finely diced onion
½ cup Pastina

1. Clean chicken and cut into serving pieces. Sauté in butter until golden brown.
2. In a 4-quart saucepan place water, salt, pepper, carrots, celery and chicken.
3. In the fat left in the frying pan sauté onion until tender and add to soup mixture. Cover and bring to boil; simmer for 30 minutes or until chicken and vegetables are tender.
4. Cook Pastina as directed on package; drain. Add to chicken. Heat thoroughly. Remove chicken to deep soup plates. Fill plates with soup.

Serves 4–6.

GENOVESE MINESTRONE *

1 quart seasoned meat stock
2 tablespoons vegetable or olive oil
¼ cup diced onion
2 cloves chopped garlic
½ cup diced celery
1 cup cooked red kidney beans

1 cup diced green unpeeled zucchini
2 cups shredded cabbage
2 cups chopped peeled tomato
1 cup shells macaroni
Grated Parmesan cheese

1. Heat the meat stock in a large casserole.
2. Sauté the onion, garlic and celery in oil and add to meat stock.
3. Add the red kidney beans, zucchini, cabbage and tomato. Simmer 10 minutes covered.
4. Cook the macaroni shells according to directions on package; drain and add. Serve sprinkled with cheese.

Serves 4–6.

*Genovese always has beans.

SEA BASS SOUP

2 cloves minced garlic
¼ cup olive oil
1 to 2 pounds sea bass
¼ bunch fresh chopped parsley

Juice of 1 fresh lemon
Salt and pepper to taste
1 cup of your favorite soup Pasta
Grated Parmesan cheese

1. Sauté garlic in oil until lightly brown.
2. Add the fish, parsley, salt and pepper to taste and the juice of the lemon. Continue cooking about 1 minute, then add enough water to cover the fish. Bring to a boil and cook until fish is just done, about 20 minutes.
3. While fish is cooking prepare Pasta according to package directions.
4. Place portions of fish and Pasta in bowls, add fish broth and sprinkle with grated Parmesan cheese.

Serves 4–6.

MEAT AND
MEAT SAUCES

Even die hard meat and potato eaters need variety in their everyday diet. Greek Pastitsio, Lamb Stroganoff, Lasagne, and Manicotti, all classic favorites plus many new exciting pasta variations with meat are included in this section.

PASTA MARUZZE SHELLS IN BACON SAUCE

½ pound bacon, diced
1 onion, sliced
1 chopped green pepper
3 tablespoons olive oil
1½ pounds fresh ripe tomatoes, peeled
   and chopped

½ teaspoon salt
¼ teaspoon crushed marjoram
¼ teaspoon pepper
1 pound Maruzze shells (large)
Grated Parmesan cheese

1. Cook bacon, onion and green pepper in oil until bacon is crisp. Add tomatoes, salt, marjoram and pepper; cook 10 minutes.
2. Cook Maruzze shells as directed on package; drain.
3. Serve sauce over cooked shells with Parmesan cheese.

Serves 4–6.

NEAPOLITAN MACARONI SAUCE

½ pound chopped beef
1 onion, sliced fine
1 clove garlic, minced
¼ cup olive oil
6 tomatoes

Salt and pepper to taste
2 cups elbow macaroni
½ pound Mozzarella cheese
Grated Parmesan cheese

1. Sauté chopped beef with onion and garlic in oil for a few minutes, stirring the meat over the pan so it takes on color. Then add the tomatoes which have been peeled and chopped. Sauté for another few minutes, then lower the fire and simmer, uncovered, stirring occasionally, until the tomatoes cook down to a thick sauce, about 10–15 minutes. Add salt and pepper to taste; thin with a little boiling water if necessary.
2. Meanwhile, cook the elbow macaroni according to directions on package; drain. At the last minute add Mozzarella cut in cubes and serve over macaroni. Sprinkle with grated Parmesan cheese.

Serves 4.

SKILLET MACARONI AND BEEF

1 pound elbow macaroni
3 tablespoons oil
¼ cup chopped onion
¼ cup chopped green pepper
1 pound ground beef

½ teaspoon salt
¼ teaspoon pepper
2 tablespoons paprika
1 (15½ ounce) jar meat sauce (or 1 pint
   of your own sauce)

1. Cook elbow macaroni following package directions; drain.
2. Heat oil in a large heavy skillet; sauté onion and green pepper 5 minutes. Add ground beef, crumbled with a fork. Cook until browned, stirring constantly. Sprinkle with salt, pepper and paprika.
3. Stir in meat sauce; blend well, and heat thoroughly. Add macaroni and cook 5 minutes longer. Taste for seasoning.

Serves 6.

MACARONI WITH BEEF AND MUSHROOM SAUCE

½ cup diced onion
2 cloves finely diced garlic
½ cup chopped parsley
1 bay leaf
6 tablespoons olive oil
1 #2½ can (3½ cups) Italian style
   peeled tomatoes
1 peppercorn
1 whole clove

Dash of nutmeg
Dash of cayenne pepper
¼ teaspoon black pepper
1½ teaspoons salt
1 cup sliced fresh mushrooms
½ pound ground beef
3 tablespoons tomato paste
1 package macaroni
½ cup grated Parmesan cheese

1. Sauté onion, garlic, parsley, and bay leaf in olive oil in saucepan.
2. Add tomatoes, peppercorn, clove, nutmeg, cayenne pepper, black pepper and salt and simmer uncovered 30 minutes. Remove bay leaf, peppercorn and whole clove. Add mushrooms.
3. Brown beef in another sauce pan and add to sauce. Add tomato paste and simmer mixture 15 minutes more.
4. Cook macaroni according to directions on package; drain. Place in serving dish. Pour sauce over macaroni. Serve with grated cheese.

Serves 4–6.

BEEF LIVER SAUCE WITH THIN SPAGHETTI

⅓ cup flour
½ teaspoon salt
1½ pounds beef liver, sliced thin
¼ cup vegetable oil
⅓ cup diced onion
1 clove finely diced garlic

1 #2½ can (3½ cups) Italian style
  peeled tomatoes
1 teaspoon salt
¼ teaspoon pepper
⅓ cup tomato paste
1 pound thin spaghetti

1. Sift flour and salt together. Dredge liver in flour. Sauté in oil until brown on both sides. Place in sauce pan with onion and garlic. Sauté for 2 minutes.
2. Add tomatoes, salt, and pepper and cover pan. Simmer 20 minutes. Add tomato paste and simmer 10 minutes or until sauce thickens.
3. Cook spaghetti according to directions on package; drain. Place in serving dish. Pour sauce over spaghetti. Arrange liver slices on top.

Serves 4–6.

CHOPPED BEEF SAUCE WITH SPAGHETTI

¼ cup diced onion
1 clove finely diced garlic
8 tablespoons olive oil
1 chopped basil leaf
¼ cup chopped parsley
2 crushed peppercorns
¼ teaspoon pepper

2 teaspoons salt
1 #2½ can (3½ cups) Italian style
  peeled tomatoes
½ pound chopped lean beef
3 tablespoons tomato paste
1 pound spaghetti
½ cup grated Parmesan cheese

1. Sauté onion and garlic in 4 tablespoons of the olive oil in heavy saucepan.
2. Add basil, parsley, peppercorns, peppers, salt and tomatoes. Simmer 30 minutes.
3. Sauté meat in remaining 4 tablespoons of the olive oil and add to sauce. Thicken with tomato paste and simmer 15 minutes more.
4. Cook spaghetti according to directions on package; drain. Place in serving dish. Pour sauce over spaghetti. Sprinkle with grated cheese.

Serves 4–6.

MOSTACCIOLI WITH BOLOGNESE SAUCE

1 sliced onion
1 minced clove garlic
2 tablespoons olive oil
½ pound ground beef
1½ pounds ripe fresh tomatoes, peeled
    and cut into chunks
¼ pound prosciutto, cut into thin strips

¼ teaspoon salt
¼ teaspoon nutmeg
Dash crushed rosemary
Dash pepper
½ cup dry red wine
8 ounces Mostaccioli
Grated Parmesan cheese

1. Sauté onion and garlic in oil until onion is tender. Stir in ground beef; cook until lightly browned. Add all remaining ingredients except Mostaccioli and cheese. Cover and simmer 15 minutes, stirring occasionally. Uncover and simmer 45 minutes, until tomatoes have cooked down, stirring occasionally.
2. Cook Mostaccioli as directed on package; drain. Serve sauce over cooked pasta and sprinkle with grated Parmesan.

Serves 4.

RIGATONI WITH CARBONARA SAUCE

1 pound Rigatoni
2 tablespoons olive oil or butter
6 slices diced bacon
⅓ cup dry white wine

3 eggs at room temperature
⅓ cup grated Parmesan cheese
⅓ cup grated Romano cheese
Freshly ground black pepper

1. Cook Rigatoni according to directions on package; drain.
2. While Rigatoni is cooking, place oil and bacon in a small skillet and sauté until bacon is crisp. Add wine and stir until it has evaporated.
3. When Rigatoni has cooked, drain and return to a hot saucepan. To it, add the eggs which have been slightly beaten with the Parmesan and Romano cheeses, plenty of black pepper and all the hot bacon fat, mixing well. This mixture will attach itself to the pasta and be cooked by its heat, so care should be taken to keep the pasta hot. If, after thorough mixing, the eggs still look raw, place the saucepan over a low flame for a minute or two, stirring constantly.

Serves 4–6.

CANNELLONI RIPIENI INFORNATI (Baked Stuffed Cannelloni)

1 pound Cannelloni

Sauce

1 medium onion
5 tablespoons olive oil
½ teaspoon salt
Dash of pepper

1 teaspoon chopped parsley
1 (6-ounce) can tomato paste
1 quart hot water

Meat Filling

½ pound chopped beef
½ pound chopped veal
2 ounces melted butter
1 tablespoon chopped parsley
1 ounce grated Parmesan cheese

½ teaspoon salt
Dash of pepper
2 beaten eggs
Grated Parmesan cheese

1. Cook Cannelloni according to directions on package; drain.
2. Preheat oven to 350 degrees.
3. Sauté onion which has been diced in olive oil. Add salt, pepper, parsley and tomato paste and allow to simmer for 5 minutes. Slowly add hot water. Stir until tomato paste is completely dissolved. Cover saucepan and simmer 20 minutes.
4. Mix meat filling in mixing bowl. Stuff the Cannelloni with the filling. Pour half of the sauce in a casserole and place stuffed Cannelloni on top; then add remainder of sauce. Sprinkle with grated Parmesan cheese. Cover pan and bake for 45 minutes.

Serves 6.

STUFFED EGGPLANT

½ cup Tubettini
1 large eggplant
¼ cup finely chopped onion
2 tablespoons vegetable oil
1 cup diced raw peeled tomatoes

1 cup ground left-over meat
½ teaspoon salt
Dash of pepper
2 tablespoons grated Parmesan cheese

1. Cook Tubettini according to directions on package; drain.
2. Preheat oven to 375 degrees.
3. Cut eggplant in half, lengthwise. Scoop out, dice pulp, leaving shell intact.
4. Sauté onion and diced eggplant pulp in oil. Add tomatoes, cover and simmer 5 minutes. Add meat, salt and pepper to cooked Tubettini. Place mixture in eggplant shell, piling it high. Sprinkle cheese on top. Place eggplant in baking pan in hot water about ⅛ inch deep. Bake in oven about 20 minutes, or until cheese is brown.

Serves 4.

BARBECUED FRANKS 'N NOODLES

¾ cup chopped onion
¼ cup chopped celery
½ cup chopped green pepper
4 tablespoons butter
1 cup catsup
⅓ cup chili sauce

3 tablespoons lemon juice
1 tablespoon soy sauce
1 pound frankfurters, sliced
4 cups noodles, cooked and drained
    (8 ounces)
1½ cups cottage cheese

1. Sauté onion, celery and green pepper in butter for 5 minutes. Add catsup, chili sauce, lemon juice and soy sauce. Cover; simmer 10 minutes. Add frankfurters; simmer 15 minutes.
2. Combine noodles and cottage cheese; cover and heat to serving temperature over low heat, stirring frequently. Spoon noodle mixture on serving platter; top with barbecued frankfurters.

Serves 8.

HAM AND MEZZANI

2 cups diced boiled ham
¼ cup chopped celery
⅓ cup chopped carrots
¼ cup chopped onion
2 tablespoons vegetable oil

1 #2½ (3½ cups) peeled tomatoes
1 teaspoon salt
Dash of pepper
⅓ cup tomato paste
1 pound Mezzani

1. Sauté ham, celery, carrots and onion in oil until brown, stirring occasionally.
2. Add tomatoes and salt and pepper. Simmer uncovered about 30 minutes. Add tomato paste and simmer until sauce thickens, about 15 minutes.
3. Cook Mezzani according to directions on package and drain. Place in serving dish. Pour sauce over Mezzani. Toss lightly.

Serves 4–6.

SPAGHETTI SPECIAL

2 tablespoons butter or margarine
1½ cups diced onions
½ cup diced leftover ham
1 can (35 ounces) plum tomatoes with
  tomato paste

Salt and pepper to taste
½ pound spaghetti

1. To prepare sauce, melt butter in large heavy saucepan. Add onions and sauté over medium heat until golden. Add ham.
2. Stir in and mash tomatoes. Simmer, covered, 20 minutes; uncover and cook 20 to 25 minutes longer or until sauce is of desired consistency. Stir occasionally. Season to taste with salt and pepper.
3. Meanwhile, cook spaghetti according to directions on package; drain. Serve with sauce.

Serves 4.

PERCIATELLI ALL'AMATRICIANA
(Ham or Bacon Sauce)

¼ pound diced prosciutto, ham or bacon
1 onion, chopped
2 tablespoons olive oil
1 (16 ounce) can tomatoes or 1 pound
    fresh tomatoes, peeled and sliced

Salt and pepper to taste
1 package Perciatelli
Grated Parmesan cheese

1. Sauté the prosciutto, ham or bacon with the onion in olive oil. (If bacon is used, omit the olive oil, then drain off all fat and add 1 tablespoon olive oil.)
2. Add the tomatoes and taste for seasoning, adding salt and pepper to taste. Simmer, uncovered for 30 minutes.
3. Cook the Perciatelli according to package directions; drain and serve covered with the sauce, and sprinkled with grated Parmesan cheese.

Serves 4–6.

BAKED MACARONI WITH HAM AND TOMATOES

1 pound Ditali
2 (11 ounce) cans condensed cream of
    chicken soup
¾ cup milk

Salt and pepper to taste
1 cup sliced ham in julienne strips
2 medium tomatoes sliced thin
2 tablespoons melted butter

1. Preheat oven to 350 degrees.
2. Cook Ditali according to directions on package; drain.
3. Combine condensed cream of chicken soup with milk, season to taste with salt and pepper and mix with macaroni.
4. Turn into a buttered casserole. Alternate overlapping slices of ham and tomatoes in a ring on top of macaroni. Drizzle a little melted butter over all and bake in oven for about 25 to 30 minutes.

Serves 4–6.

MACARONI AND HAM CASSEROLE

2 cups elbow macaroni	2 cups hot milk
2 cups cooked smoked ham	1 teaspoon salt
1 cup green peas	Dash of pepper
2 sliced hard boiled eggs	½ teaspoon dry mustard
¼ cup butter or margarine	½ teaspoon Worcestershire sauce
¼ cup flour	½ cup breadcrumbs, buttered

1. Cook macaroni according to directions on package; drain.
2. Preheat oven to 350 degrees.
3. Dice ham and mix with macaroni. Cook green peas and mix with macaroni. Add eggs and mix well.
4. Make white sauce of the butter, flour, milk and seasonings and lightly stir into elbows. Place mixture in 1½ quart greased casserole.
5. Cover elbows with breadcrumbs. Bake for 30 minutes or until crumbs are brown.

Serves 4.

FRESH TOMATOES WITH HAMBURGERS AND MACARONI

2 cups elbow macaroni	¼ cup chopped parsley
⅔ pound chopped beef	¼ cup vegetable oil
⅓ pound chopped pork	2 pounds (4 cups) diced raw tomatoes
1 teaspoon salt	1 teaspoon salt
Dash of pepper	¼ cup grated Parmesan cheese

1. Cook elbow macaroni according to directions on package; drain.
2. Preheat oven to 400 degrees.
3. Mix together meat, salt, pepper and parsley. Form into 8 small patties. Sauté patties in oil until brown.
4. Combine tomatoes, 1 teaspoon salt and cooked elbows with patties. Place in a 2 quart casserole. Bake in oven for 40 minutes.
5. Sprinkle top with cheese. Bake 10 minutes or until cheese is brown.

Serves 4–6.

CURRIED LAMB WITH EGG NOODLES

¼ cup butter or margarine
¼ cup flour
2 teaspoons curry powder
2 cups hot seasoned beef broth
½ teaspoon salt

Dash of pepper
3 cups diced cooked lamb
1 cup cooked peas
½ pound wide egg noodles

1. Melt butter or margarine in frying pan and stir in flour and curry powder.
2. Add beef broth and salt and pepper. Simmer until sauce thickens, stirring constantly; add diced lamb and peas. Simmer about 10 minutes.
3. Cook egg noodles according to directions on package; drain. Place in a serving dish. Pour meat and sauce over noodles. Toss lightly.

Serves 4–6.

LAMB STROGANOFF WITH NOODLES

¼ cup flour
1 teaspoon salt
¼ teaspoon pepper
1½ pounds boneless lamb shoulder, thinly sliced
6 tablespoons butter
1 clove garlic, minced
½ pound sliced mushrooms

1 onion, diced fine
¼ cup tomato sauce
¼ cup water
1 teaspoon caraway seed
1 (3 ounce) package cream cheese, softened
1 cup sour cream
1 (12 ounce) package egg noodles

1. Combine flour, salt and pepper; coat meat with this mixture. In a large skillet, melt 4 tablespoons of the butter; add garlic and meat. Brown meat slowly, tossing occasionally to brown on all sides. Remove meat from skillet and add the remaining butter. Add mushrooms and onion; sauté 3 to 5 minutes. Return meat to skillet; stir in tomato sauce, water and caraway seed. Cover and simmer for 15 to 20 minutes, or until meat is tender. Blend in cream cheese and sour cream just before serving; do not boil, just heat to serving temperature.
2. Meanwhile, cook noodles according to directions on package; drain. Serve Stroganoff on top.

Serves 6.

LASAGNE IMBOTTITE (Baked Lasagne)

Sauce

1 small diced onion
1 clove garlic, chopped
¼ cup olive oil
1 #2½ can Italian tomatoes

1 can tomato paste
1 tablespoon chopped parsley
3 basil leaves
Salt and pepper to taste

Meatballs

½ pound chopped ground beef
¼ cup breadcrumbs
2 tablespoons chopped parsley
⅛ cup milk

1 beaten egg
3 tablespoons grated cheese
Salt and pepper to taste
2 tablespoons olive oil

Lasagne

1 pound Lasagne
1 pound Mozzarella cheese

1 pound Ricotta cheeese
4 ounces grated Parmesan cheese

1. Sauté the onion and garlic in the olive oil in a saucepan. Add the tomatoes, tomato paste, parsley, basil, salt and pepper to taste and let sauce simmer for 15 minutes.
2. Mix all meatball ingredients except the olive oil thoroughly. Shape into tiny meatballs, the size of marbles. Brown in frying pan with olive oil and then add to saucepan with sauce. Simmer mixture uncovered 30 minutes.
3. Preheat oven to 350 degrees.
4. While sauce is simmering cook Lasagne according to directions on package; drain well.
5. Using a baking dish about 2 inches deep arrange casserole with several spoonsful sauce on bottom, then place a layer of Lasagne, cover with several slices of Mozzarella, 4 or 5 tablespoons Ricotta, sprinkle with some of the grated cheese and spread about ¼ of the sauce and meatballs. Repeat ending with a layer of Lasagne and the sauce. Bake 20 minutes.

Serves 6.

LEFT-OVER MEAT SAUCE WITH SHELLS

2½ cups medium shell macaroni
¼ cup chopped onion
3 cups diced cold left-over roast
¼ cup vegetable oil
⅔ cup (6 ounce can) tomato paste
2 cups seasoned beef broth

1 teaspoon dry mustard
½ teaspoon salt
Dash of pepper
2 tablespoons finely chopped
   celery leaves
2 tablespoons chopped parsley

1. Cook shells according to directions on package; drain.
2. Sauté onion and meat in oil until brown in sauce pot.
3. Add tomato paste, beef broth, mustard, salt, pepper, celery and parsley and simmer for about 30 minutes. Place cooked shells in serving dish. Pour sauce over shells. Toss lightly.
Serves 4.

EASY BAKED LASAGNE

2 (15½ ounce) jars prepared meat,
   meatless or mushroom sauce
½ cup water
1 pound ribbed Lasagne
1 pound Ricotta cheese

¾ cup grated cheese
1 egg
1 pound skim milk Mozzarella cheese,
   sliced

1. Preheat oven to 375 degrees.
2. Combine sauce with water and heat.
3. Cook ribbed Lasagne, following package directions; drain; rinse in cold water; drain again.
4. Combine Ricotta with 2 tablespoons of the grated cheese and the egg; mix well.
5. Spread a thin layer of sauce in the bottom of a rectangular pan. Arrange Lasagne strips, side by side, spreading each with Ricotta mixture. Cover with slices of Mozzarella. Top with a layer of sauce and a sprinkling of grated cheese. Bake in oven for about 30–40 minutes.
Serves 4–6.

Variations:

To enrich this basic recipe, any of the following or a combination of them, may be added to the layers; tiny meatballs, cooked peas, cut-up cooked sausages or sliced hard-boiled eggs.

STRACOTTO (EXTRA COOKED)
MEAT SAUCE WITH PASTA

1 ounce dried mushrooms
1 pound top sirloin or top round (all lean)
1 medium onion
1 medium carrot
1 stalk celery
1 bunch parsley
½ cup butter

½ cup dry Marsala or Madeira wine
½ cup beef bouillon
Salt and pepper to taste
1 teaspoon grated lemon rind
1 pound pasta
Grated Parmesan cheese

1. Soak the dried mushrooms in tepid water for half an hour, then drain and chop.
2. Trim the meat of all fat and tendons, etc., and dice.
3. Mince the onion, carrot, celery and parsley together.
4. Heat the butter in a heavy saucepan, add the minced onion, carrot, celery and parsley and sauté for a few minutes, stirring frequently. Then add the diced beef and continue cooking for another 5 minutes, until everything is golden and buttery. Add the wine, the bouillon and the dried mushrooms, salt and pepper, and stir in the grated lemon rind.
5. Cover tightly and simmer over the lowest possible fire (preferably on an asbestos pad) until the meat is "stracotto" — extra cooked, almost dissolved into the sauce. This takes 3 to 4 hours, depending on the meat, and the long cooking is essential for flavor and the proper thick consistency.
6. Cook pasta according to directions on the package; drain and serve covered with the sauce. (Any pasta will do.) Add grated Parmesan to taste.

Serves 4–6.

MACARONI MEAT LOAF

2 cups elbow macaroni
¼ cup chopped onions
1 tablespoon chopped parsley
¼ cup chopped green pepper
2 tablespoons vegetable oil
1 cup beef broth

2 beaten eggs
1 teaspoon salt
1 teaspoon dry mustard
1 tablespoon horseradish
¾ pound chopped beef
¼ pound chopped pork

1. Cook elbow macaroni according to directions on package; drain.
2. Preheat oven to 350 degrees.
3. Sauté onions, parsley and green pepper in vegetable oil.
4. Blend beef broth, eggs, salt, dry mustard and horseradish together. Combine beef and pork with all ingredients, including elbows, mixing well. Place in greased loaf pan. Bake in oven one hour until firm.

Serves 4–6.

SPAGHETTI AND MEAT SAUCE

¾ medium onion, sliced or diced
¼ cup olive oil or butter
½ pound lean ground beef
½ pound lean ground pork
2 (8-ounce) cans tomato sauce
1 (6-ounce) can tomato paste
1 teaspoon fresh or ¼ teaspoon
  dried parsley

⅓ green pepper, sliced or diced
¼ teaspoon oregano
¼ teaspoon basil
1 teaspoon salt
Freshly ground black pepper to taste
1 pound Spaghettini (thin spaghetti)
Grated Parmesan cheese

1. Brown onion in the olive oil or butter until golden. Add meat and brown. Add tomato sauce and paste and stir well. Add parsley, green pepper, oregano, basil, salt and pepper, and simmer for 15 minutes, stirring occasionally.
2. Cook Spaghettini according to directions on package; drain. Serve sauce over hot, cooked Spaghettini and sprinkle generously with grated Parmesan cheese.

Serves 4–6.

FRANKFURTERS AND SHELL MACARONI

1 pound frankfurters
½ cup finely chopped onion
¼ cup vegetable oil
1 (6 ounce) can tomato paste

1 teaspoon salt
Dash of pepper
2 cups hot water
2½ cups shell macaroni

1. Slice frankfurters very thin. Sauté with onion in vegetable oil.
2. Add tomato paste, salt, pepper and water and simmer for 20 minutes or until sauce thickens.
3. Cook shells according to directions on package; drain. Place in serving dish. Pour sauce over shells. Toss lightly.

Serves 4.

MEAT BALLS AND MOSTACCIOLI

Meat Balls

½ pound ground beef
½ pound ground pork or veal
2 slightly beaten eggs
Salt and pepper to taste
2 tablespoons chopped parsley

½ cup breadcrumbs
2 tablespoons grated Parmesan cheese
2 tablespoons chopped onion
¼ cup olive oil

Sauce

¼ cup chopped onions
1-pound can tomatoes
1 (6 ounce) can tomato paste
¼ teaspoon basil

¼ teaspoon oregano
Salt and pepper to taste
1 pound Mostaccioli
Grated Parmesan cheese

1. Combine meat, eggs, salt and pepper in a mixing bowl. Add parsley, breadcrumbs, Parmesan cheese and onion, mixing thoroughly. Shape into one inch balls and brown in olive oil until well done. Remove meat balls from pan and set aside.
2. Next, make the sauce by browning chopped onions in meat ball drippings. When done, add tomatoes, tomato paste, basil, oregano, salt and pepper and simmer slowly for about 10 minutes. Return meat balls to sauce and heat to serving temperature.
3. Meanwhile, cook Mostaccioli according to directions on package; drain. Serve sauce over Mostaccioli with a little extra Parmesan.

Serves 4–6.

VERMICELLI WITH BRAISED PORK CHOPS

¼ cup flour
½ teaspoon salt
4 rib pork chops 1¼ inch thick
2 tablespoons vegetable oil
1 sliced onion
1 #2½ can (3½ cups) Italian Style
   peeled tomatoes

3 tablespoons tomato paste
1 teaspoon salt
¼ teaspoon pepper
1 pound Vermicelli
¼ cup grated Parmesan cheese

1. Blend flour and salt together. Dredge pork chops in flour. Sauté chops until brown. Place in saucepan.
2. Add onion, tomatoes, tomato paste, salt and pepper. Cook, covered, over low heat 30 minutes, stirring occasionally.
3. Cook Vermicelli according to directions on package; drain. Place in serving dish. Pour sauce over Vermicelli. Arrange chops on top. Serve with grated cheese.

Serves 4–6.

MACARONI NGOW-YOK
(Chinese Macaroni with Ground Beef)

4 ounces elbow macaroni
1 pound ground beef
¼ cup chopped onion
1 clove finely chopped garlic
4 diced medium tomatoes
2 tablespoons vegetable oil
Salt and pepper to taste

1 cup beef broth
1 cup chopped celery
⅔ cup chopped green pepper
2 tablespoons corn starch
2 teaspoons soy sauce
¼ cup water

1. Cook elbow macaroni according to directions on package; drain.
2. Sauté beef, onion, garlic and tomatoes in oil. Add salt and pepper. Cook over moderate heat for 5 minutes, stirring constantly. Add beef broth, celery and green pepper. Cover pan and cook 5 minutes.
3. Blend together corn starch, soy sauce, and water and add. Cook until sauce thickens. Serve very hot over cooked elbows.

Serves 4.

GREEK PASTITSIO

1 pound elbow macaroni
¼ cup melted butter
1½ cups grated Parmesan cheese
3 eggs, beaten

1 cup milk
1 pound ground beef
1 cup tomato sauce

Bechamel Sauce

3 tablespoons butter
3 tablespoons flour
3 cups milk

¾ cup cream
3 egg yolks, lightly beaten

1. Preheat oven to 350 degrees.
2. Cook elbow macaroni according to directions on package; drain.
3. Pour melted butter over the macaroni, sprinkle with ¾ cup Parmesan cheese and blend. Combine eggs and milk. Add to macaroni and mix thoroughly.
4. Brown meat, breaking up the lumps. Cook about 10 minutes and add tomato sauce. Set aside.
5. To prepare Bechamel Sauce, melt butter in saucepan and stir in flour. Add milk and cook, stirring until the mixture is thickened and smooth. Combine the cream with the egg yolks and blend. Stir this into sauce and heat thoroughly, but do not boil or mixture will curdle.
6. In a buttered 9″×13″×2″ pan, make a layer of macaroni, a layer of meat and another layer of macaroni. Cover with sauce and sprinkle with remaining Parmesan cheese. Bake for about 40 minutes.
7. After removing from oven, allow to stand until warm. Slice into large squares and serve.
Serves 6–8.

SAUSAGE CASSEROLE WITH ELBOW MACARONI

½ pound link pork sausage
½ cup water
¼ cup chopped green pepper
¼ cup chopped onion

1 can (1¼ cups) condensed undiluted
   tomato soup
2 cups elbow macaroni

1. Preheat oven to 350 degrees.
2. Place sausage and water in covered frying pan. Cook until tender — about 20 minutes. Remove sausage from pan.
3. Add green pepper and onion and sauté for 5 minutes. Add tomato soup and heat.
4. Cook elbow macaroni according to directions on package; drain. Add and stir thoroughly. Place elbows and sauce in 1½ quart greased casserole. Arrange sausage on top. Bake about 30 minutes.

Serves 4.

SAUSAGE-TOMATO SAUCE WITH SPAGHETTI

1 pound Italian sweet sausage
1 medium green pepper, cut into strips
½ sliced onion
1 (1-pound 12 ounce) can plum tomatoes
1 (6-ounce) can tomato paste

½ teaspoon dried basil
¼ teaspoon salt
Dash of pepper
1 pound spaghetti
Grated Parmesan cheese

1. Brown sausage in a saucepan for 10 to 15 minutes. Remove sausage and drain off all but 1 tablespoon of the fat. Add the green pepper and cook about 5 minutes. Remove with a spoon and reserve. Next cook the onion until browned slightly. Then stir in tomatoes, tomato paste, basil, salt and pepper. Add the sausage and simmer all together very slowly for 15–20 minutes. Return the green pepper to the mixture for the last 10 minutes.
2. Cook spaghetti according to directions on package; drain.
3. Serve sauce, sprinkled with Parmesan cheese, over cooked pasta.

Serves 4–6.

STUFFED TOMATOES

1 cup Orzo
4 large ripe tomatoes
¼ cup chopped onion
¼ cup chopped celery

2 tablespoons vegetable oil
½ cup chopped cooked leftover meat
½ teaspoon salt
Dash of pepper

1. Cook Orzo according to directions on package; drain.
2. Preheat oven to 375 degrees.
3. From the top of each tomato cut a slice ½ inch thick. Scoop out center and dice tomato pulp.
4. Sauté onion and celery in oil. Add cooked Orzo and tomato pulp.
5. Add meat and salt and pepper to onion and celery mixture. Fill tomato cups with the complete mixture, cover tops with the ½ inch tomato slice. Place in shallow baking dish with ¼ inch hot water. Bake in oven about 25 minutes or until tender.

Serves 4.

ZUCCHINI LASAGNE

2 tablespoons butter
1 pound ground beef
½ cup chopped onion
1 (15 ounce) can tomato sauce
½ cup water
¼ cup teaspoon salt

¼ teaspoon oregano
7 Lasagne strips, cooked and drained
¾ cup grated Parmesan cheese
2 tablespoons flour
4 cups zucchini slices
12 ounces Mozzarella cheese, sliced

1. Preheat oven to 375 degrees.
2. Melt butter in a large skillet. Brown beef with onions; drain. Stir in tomato sauce, water and seasonings. Cover and simmer 30 minutes, stirring occasionally.
3. Combine Parmesan cheese and flour. Layer half the Lasagne strips on bottom of buttered 13½ × 8¾ inch baking dish. Top with half the zucchini, half the Parmesan mixture, half the meat sauce and half the Mozzarella cheese. Repeat layers of Lasagne, zucchini, Parmesan mixture and meat sauce. Bake in oven for 20–25 minutes or until zucchini is tender. Add remaining Mozzarella cheese to top; return to oven until cheese begins to melt. Let stand 10 minutes before serving.

Serves 6.

POULTRY
WITH PASTA

What could be more versatile than chicken? Combine that with macaroni, noodles and spaghetti and you'll have an infinite variety of tempting main courses. We've all heard of Chicken Cacciatore but why not try Chicken Tetrazzini with Spaghetti or Chicken with Noodle stuffing for a change.

STUFFING FOR ROAST CHICKEN
(for a 4–5 pound roasting chicken)

1 cup Tubettini (small tubular macaroni)
¼ cup finely chopped onion
¼ cup finely chopped celery
1 cup sliced mushrooms
Cooked chopped chicken giblets
3 tablespoons vegetable oil or chicken fat

½ cup chopped parsley
1 teaspoon salt
Dash of pepper
½ teaspoon sage
1 beaten egg

1. Cook Tubettini according to directions on package; drain.
2. Sauté onions, celery, mushrooms and giblets in oil.
3. Add parsley, salt, pepper, sage and egg. Then add Tubettini. Mix thoroughly. Stuff chicken and roast as you would ordinarily do.

EASY CHICKEN CACCIATORE WITH NOODLES

1 (2½ pound) chicken, cut into
  serving pieces
3 tablespoons oil
1 small finely chopped onion
2 cloves minced garlic

1 (15½ ounce) jar marinara sauce
12 ounces fine egg noodles
¼ cup grated Parmesan cheese
1 tablespoon chopped parsley

1. Remove skin from chicken pieces. Heat oil in a large skillet and lightly brown chicken.
2. Add onion and garlic; continue cooking until golden brown and onion lightly colored, about 15 minutes.
3. Stir in marinara sauce. Cover and simmer for about 25 minutes, or until chicken is tender.
4. Cook noodles, following package directions; drain.
5. Lift chicken pieces from sauce; mix noodles with sauce and grated Parmesan cheese. Top with chicken pieces and sprinkle with parsley.
Serves 4–6.

65

CHICKEN AND NOODLES

½ pound medium egg noodles
¼ cup chopped green pepper
4 tablespoons chopped onion
1 cup sliced mushrooms
4 tablespoons vegetable oil
4 tablespoons flour

2 cups hot chicken broth
½ teaspoon salt
Dash of pepper
1 tablespoon chopped parsley
2 cups diced cooked chicken
¼ teaspoon paprika

1. Cook egg noodles according to directions on package; drain.
2. Sauté green pepper, onion and mushroom in oil.
3. Stir in flour. Add chicken broth gradually, cooking until thickened.
4. Add salt and pepper, parsley and chicken to the thickened sauce. Stir cooked noodles in lightly. Cook covered until very hot.
5. Garnish with paprika and serve.

Serves 4.

CHICKEN CACCIATORE A LA CASALINGA*

1 (4 pound) chicken cut in pieces
½ cup flour
1 teaspoon salt
½ cup vegetable shortening
¼ cup chopped onion
1 clove finely chopped garlic
¼ cup chopped carrot

A few sprigs parsley
1 basil or bay leaf
3½ cups tomatoes
1 teaspoon salt
1 teaspoon pepper
¼ cup sherry or white wine
½ pound medium egg noodles

1. Sift together flour and salt; dredge chicken. Sauté in vegetable oil until brown. Place in covered dish and keep hot.
2. Sauté onion, garlic, carrot, parsley and basil or bay leaf in same oil used to cook chicken.
3. Strain tomatoes, using pulp only (about 2 cups). Add tomatoes, salt and pepper to sautéed vegetables. Bring to a boil.
4. Add chicken and wine. Simmer covered until chicken is tender, about 30 minutes.
5. Cook egg noodles according to directions on package; drain and place in serving dish. Pour sauce over noodles. Toss lightly. Arrange chicken on top.

Serves 4–6.

*Note: Cacciatora means ''Hunter'' style — with wine, garlic, subtle herbs, and, usually, onions and tomatoes. A la Casalinga means homemade.

66

CHICKEN AND MACARONI CASSEROLE

1 cup elbow macaroni
2 cups cooked diced chicken
1½ tablespoons grated onion
⅔ cup chopped green pepper
1 cup cooked diced carrots

¼ teaspoon paprika
1½ teaspoons salt
Dash of pepper
2 eggs, slightly beaten
1½ cups milk

1. Preheat oven to 350 degrees.
2. Cook elbow macaroni according to directions on package; drain.
3. Combine chicken, onion, green pepper, carrots, paprika salt and pepper with cooked macaroni and place in greased 1½ quart casserole.
4. Combine eggs and milk and pour into casserole. Set in pan of hot water and bake about one hour, or until firm.

Serves 4.

CHICKEN CREOLE WITH NOODLES

4 tablespoons butter
1 cup chopped onion
½ cup chopped celery
½ cup chopped green pepper
1 pound can tomatoes
1 teaspoon salt
1 teaspoon chili powder

Dash of pepper
½ cup milk
2 tablespoons flour
2 cups chopped cooked chicken
1 12 ounce package noodles
1 cup shredded Cheddar cheese

1. In a 2-quart saucepan melt butter; sauté onion, celery and green pepper until tender. Add tomatoes, salt, chili powder and pepper; cover and simmer 15 minutes.
2. Meanwhile, in a small bowl combine milk and flour, stirring until smooth. Gradually add milk mixture to tomato sauce; cook over medium heat, stirring constantly until thickened. Cook 2 additional minutes. Add chicken; cover and heat over low heat, stirring occasionally.
3. At the same time cook noodles according to directions on the package; drain and mix with butter.
4. Add cheese to creole; stir until cheese is melted. Serve over noodles.

Makes 6 servings.

CHICKEN LIVER SAUCE WITH RIGATONI

2 cups finely chopped onion
6 slices bacon, cut up
¼ cup butter or margarine
½ pound chicken livers, cut up
2 finely chopped green peppers
½ cup minced parsley

2 teaspoons salt
½ teaspoon pepper
1 (1-pound 12-ounce) can Italian tomatoes
¼ cup dry red wine
½ pound sliced fresh mushrooms
1 pound Rigatoni (ribbed macaroni)

1. Cook onion and bacon in butter or margarine until bacon is crisp. Add chicken livers; cook 5 minutes. Stir in green pepper, parsley, salt and pepper. Cover and simmer 10 minutes. Add tomatoes and wine; heat to boiling. Add mushrooms; reduce heat and simmer 20 minutes, stirring occasionally.
2. Cook Rigatoni as directed on package; drain. Serve sauce over cooked Rigatoni.
Serves 4–6.

CHICKEN SPINACH NOODLE CASSEROLE

4 cups spinach egg noodles, cooked and
    drained (8 ounces uncooked)
2 tablespoons butter
Dash of pepper
1 broiler-frying chicken, about 3 pounds
    cut up

1 (10¾ ounce) can cream of celery soup
¾ cup milk
½ cup grated Parmesan cheese
2 tablespoons chopped chives
Paprika
1 (16 ounce) can whole carrots, drained

1. Preheat oven to 350 degrees.
2. Toss together noodles, butter and pepper; spoon into buttered 13½ x 8¾ inch baking dish. Place chicken on noodles. Combine soup, milk, ¼ cup Parmesan cheese and chives; pour over chicken. Sprinkle with remaining cheese and paprika.
3. Bake in oven for 45 minutes; add carrots. Bake 15 to 20 minutes longer or until chicken is tender.
Makes 4–6 servings.

CREAMED CHICKEN MOLD

2 cups elbow macaroni
3 tablespoons butter or margarine
3 tablespoons flour
1½ cups milk

¾ teaspoon salt
Dash of pepper
2 eggs
3 cups creamed chicken

1. Cook elbow macaroni according to directions on package; drain.
2. Preheat oven to 350 degrees.
3. Prepare white sauce by mixing butter or margarine and flour over low heat and then gradually adding milk, salt and pepper, stirring constantly. Then cool slightly.
4. Beat eggs. Pour sauce over eggs, stirring constantly. Mix with elbow macaroni. Place in a one quart well greased ring mold. Place mold in pan of hot water. Bake 30 minutes until firm. Unmold on serving dish.
5. Fill center with creamed chicken which has been heated

Serves 4–6.

MEDITERRANEAN CHICKEN AND MUSHROOM SAUCE WITH FETTUCCINE

¾ cup cooked chicken, in strips
½ cup white mushrooms sliced thin
½ cup heavy cream

Salt and pepper to taste
½ pound Fettuccine
½ cup grated Parmesan cheese

1. Combine thin strips of cooked chicken, mushrooms and cream in a deep skillet. Add salt and pepper to taste.
2. Simmer gently until thoroughly hot, but do not boil.
3. Meanwhile cook Fettuccine according to directions on package; drain.
4. Remove sauce from heat; add hot, drained Fettuccine and mix well. Sprinkle with grated Parmesan cheese, mix once more and serve.

Serves 2–4.

CHICKEN AND MUSHROOM ALMOND VERMICELLI

1 (6 ounce) can sliced mushrooms or
  ½ pound fresh mushrooms
3 tablespoons butter
1½ cup chopped or cut up cooked
  left-over chicken

2 cups chicken broth or bouillon
Salt and pepper to taste
1 pound Vermicelli
¼ cup slivered toasted almonds
Grated Parmesan cheese

1. Sauté mushrooms in butter for about 3 minutes; add chicken and chicken broth or bouillon; season to taste with salt and pepper. Heat through.
2. Meanwhile, cook Vermicelli according to directions on package; drain, and heap on serving dish, topping with mushroom and chicken mixture. Sprinkle generously with slivered toasted almonds. Serve with grated cheese if desired.

Serves 4–6.

CHICKEN TETRAZZINI*

¼ pound fresh mushrooms
¼ cup butter
¼ cup flour
1 slice pimiento, cut thin
½ teaspoon salt
Dash black pepper
¼ teaspoon paprika

1½ cups milk
½ cup rich chicken stock or 1 bouillon
  cube and additional ½ cup milk
8 ounces Vermicelli
2 cups shredded chicken
⅓ cup grated Parmesan cheese
1 tablespoon chopped parsley

1. Preheat oven to 350 degrees.
2. Slice mushrooms and sauté in butter.
3. Add flour, pimiento, salt, pepper, paprika, milk and chicken stock and allow to simmer, stirring constantly until it thickens. Remove from heat.
4. Break Vermicelli into lengths about 3 inches each. Cook according to directions on package and drain.
5. Blend chicken with sauce and Vermicelli. Spread in buttered baking dish.
6. Sprinkle grated cheese thickly over mixture. Brown in oven for 20 minutes. Garnish with parsley.

Serves 4.

*(Chicken Tetrazzini was named after the famous coloratura who reigned supreme in opera during the early years of this century. She adored pasta and this dish was created for her in San Francisco where she loved to sing . . . and to eat.)

CHICKEN TETRAZZINI WITH PEAS AND PASTA

3 tablespoons butter
⅓ cup diced onion
3 tablespoons flour
1 envelope instant chicken broth mix or
   bouillon cube, crushed
¼ teaspoon dried savory
Dash of pepper
1 cup milk (approximately)

1½ cups diced cooked chicken or turkey
1 (3 or 4-ounce) can mushrooms, drained,
   with liquid reserved
1 #2 can peas, drained
2 tablespoons grated Parmesan cheese
Salt to taste
8 ounces Maruzzelle shells

1. Melt butter, add onion and cook slightly. Quickly stir in flour, broth, savory and pepper. Blend until smooth and remove from heat.
2. Combine reserved mushroom liquid with enough milk to measure 2 cups, and add to flour mixture, a little at a time, stirring constantly. Boil 1 minute. Then stir in chicken, mushrooms, peas, cheese and salt to taste. Heat to serving temperature.
3. Cook Maruzzelle shells as directed on package; drain. Serve sauce over cooked shells with a little extra grated Parmesan cheese.

Serves 4.

FISH AND FISH SAUCES WITH PASTA

Using pasta as an extender can help to make fish dishes economical despite the current high price of fish. A shrimp creole with macaroni, a seafood casserole, or spaghetti with clam sauce can happily feed many appreciative mouths.

ROTINI WITH RED CLAM SAUCE

1 clove garlic, minced
1 cup butter
¾ cup olive oil
2 (8-ounce) cans minced clams, undrained
2 (10½ ounce) cans tomato puree
½ cup finely chopped parsley

1 teaspoon crushed basil
½ teaspoon oregano
1 teaspoon crushed red pepper
¼ teaspoon black pepper
1 pound Rotini

1. Cook garlic in butter and olive oil until lightly browned. Add remaining ingredients except Rotini. Simmer 20 minutes, stirring occasionally.
2. Cook Rotini as directed on package; drain. Serve sauce over cooked Rotini.
Serves 4–6.

LITTLE NECK CLAM SAUCE WITH LINGUINE

2 dozen Little Neck clams
2 tablespoons chopped parsley
3½ cups Italian Style peeled tomatoes
1½ teaspoons salt
¼ teaspoon pepper

½ clove garlic
¼ cup olive oil
⅓ cup tomato paste
1 pound Linguine

1. Wash clams and steam. When open remove clams from shells. Chop and set aside.
2. Simmer parsley, tomatoes, salt and pepper uncovered for 30 minutes.
3. Sauté garlic in oil and add. Add tomato paste and simmer 15 minutes uncovered. Add chopped clams. Simmer 2 minutes more.
4. Cook Linguine according to directions on package; drain. Place in serving dish. Pour clam sauce over Linguine.
Serves 4–6.

WINE CLAM SAUCE WITH SPAGHETTINI

½ onion
a handful parsley
1 clove garlic
¼ cup olive oil
2 tablespoons butter

1 (8-ounce) can minced clams
½ cup dry white wine
Pepper to taste
1 pound cooked Spaghettini

1. Chop the onion finely. Sauté with the parsley and garlic in olive oil and butter until golden.
2. Add the minced clams with their juice and let simmer for a few minutes.
3. Add the dry white wine, simmer for 2 or 3 minutes more. Add pepper, and serve over hot, drained thin spaghetti (Spaghettini).

Serves 4–6.

LINGUINE WITH WHITE CLAM SAUCE

1 package (1 pound) Linguine
3 tablespoons vegetable oil
3 cloves minced garlic
1 dozen cherrystone clams and
   their juice (fresh, jarred, or canned)

¼ cup chopped parsley
Salt and pepper to taste
Grated cheese

1. Cook Linguine following package directions; drain.
2. Heat oil in a saucepan and lightly brown garlic. Add the clams and their juice, parsley, and salt and pepper to taste. Simmer gently for about 5 minutes. Pour sauce over Linguine and toss.

Serve with grated cheese. Serves 4–6.

Variation:

For a red clam sauce, add 1 cup Marinara sauce to oil and garlic and bring to a simmer before adding clams and parsley.

COD FISH SAUCE WITH SPAGHETTI

2 pounds cod fish
1 bay leaf
½ cup water
⅓ cup diced onion
1 clove finely diced garlic
⅓ cup vegetable or olive oil

3½ cups Italian style peeled tomatoes
1½ teaspoons salt
Dash of pepper
3 tablespoons tomato paste
1 pound spaghetti

1. Simmer cod, bay leaf and water in saucepan 10 minutes. Remove fish. Cut in small cubes and set aside.
2. Sauté onion and garlic in oil and add to fish soup in saucepan.
3. Add tomatoes, salt and pepper, and tomato paste. Simmer 30 minutes uncovered or until sauce thickens. Then add cubed fish.
4. Cook spaghetti according to the directions on the package; drain. Pour sauce with cod over spaghetti in serving dish.

Serves 4–6.

CREOLE FISH FILLETS WITH NOODLES

8 ounces medium egg noodles
   (about 4 cups)
2 tablespoons vegetable oil
½ cup chopped onions
1 pound-can tomatoes
1 (6-ounce) can tomato paste
1 teaspoon garlic salt

¼ teaspoon oregano
¼ teaspoon pepper
2 packages (1 pound each) frozen
   fish fillets, thawed (halibut, haddock,
   cod) or fresh fish fillets

1. Cook noodles according to the directions on the package; drain.
2. Meanwhile, heat oil in heavy skillet. Add onions and cook over low heat 5 minutes.
3. Add undrained tomatoes, tomato paste, garlic salt, oregano and pepper; mix well. Heat to boiling point.
4. Roll fish fillets and secure with toothpicks. Add to sauce; cover and cook over low heat 10 minutes.
5. Turn rolled fillets and stir tomato mixture. Cover and cook 10 minutes longer.

Serve with noodles. Garnish with parsley, and lemon slices, if desired. Serves 6.

CREOLE SHRIMP SAUCE WITH NOODLES

¼ cup diced onion
¼ cup diced green pepper
2 tablespoons olive oil
2 tablespoons flour
2½ cups tomato purée

1 teaspoon salt
Dash of pepper
1 (4 ounce) can shrimp
⅔ cup evaporated milk
½ pound wide egg noodles

1. Sauté onion and green pepper in oil.
2. Add flour and stir thoroughly. Then add tomato purée, salt and pepper and cook until sauce thickens. Add shrimp. Heat thoroughly and remove. Add milk gradually, stirring constantly.
3. Cook noodles according to directions on package; drain. Place in serving dish. Pour sauce over noodles. Arrange shrimp on top.

Serves 4.

LOBSTER SAUCE WITH SPAGHETTI

1 large boiled lobster
3½ cups Italian style peeled tomatoes
1½ teaspoons salt
2 tablespoons chopped parsley
¼ teaspoon pepper

¼ cup diced onion
¼ cup olive or vegetable oil
⅓ cup tomato paste
1 pound Spaghettini (thin spaghetti)

1. Remove lobster from shell and chop in large pieces
2. Simmer tomatoes, parsley, salt and pepper uncovered for 30 minutes in casserole.
3. Sauté onion in oil. Add tomato paste and onion to tomato mixture and cook 15 minutes more or until sauce thickens. Add chopped lobster and simmer 10 minutes more.
4. Cook Spaghettini according to directions on package; drain. Place in serving dish. Pour lobster sauce on top.

Serves 4–6.

MACARONI SALMON LOAF

1 cup Ditalini
1 pound cooked salmon
1 tablespoon grated onion
¼ cup diced green pepper
2 tablespoons chopped parsley

⅓ cup milk
2 eggs
1 teaspoon salt
Dash of pepper
1 pint white sauce

1. Preheat the oven to 350 degrees.
2. Cook Ditalini according to the directions on the package; drain.
3. Mix the salmon, onion, green pepper and parsley and add to the Ditalini.
4. Blend the milk, eggs, salt and pepper and add to Ditalini. Mix thoroughly. Place in a greased loaf pan. Bake until firm about 50 minutes. Serve with a medium thick white sauce.

Serves 4–6.

SCALLOPED OYSTERS WITH ELBOW MACARONI

1 tablespoon grated onion
¼ cup vegetable oil
2 tablespoons flour
1 cup hot milk
¼ cup oyster juice

½ teaspoon salt
Dash of pepper
2 cups elbow macaroni
1 pint oysters, cleaned
½ cup bread crumbs

1. Sauté onion in vegetable oil.
2. Preheat oven to 350 degrees.
3. Add flour, milk, oyster juice, salt and pepper and simmer over low heat. Stir until it thickens.
4. Cook elbow macaroni according to directions on package; drain. In a greased 1½ quart casserole place ⅓ elbows, ½ oysters and another layer of elbows; the rest of the oysters and the remainder of the elbows. Add the sauce. Cover with bread crumbs. Bake in oven 30 minutes.

Serves 4.

SCALLOPS AND MARUZZELLE

1 egg
2 tablespoons cold water
1 pound (1 pint) bay scallops
½ cup fine bread crumbs
6 tablespoons vegetable oil
⅓ cup sliced scallion

1 teaspoon salt
Dash of pepper
1 cup chicken broth
¼ cup flour
3 cups Maruzzelle (medium shells)
⅓ cup grated Parmesan cheese

1. Mix egg and water and beat slightly.
2. Wash scallops and simmer for 5 minutes in egg and water. Drain and reserve liquid. Roll in egg and then in bread crumbs.
3. Saute scallops in oil until golden brown. Remove from frying pan. Sauté scallion in frying pan until tender. Add water in which scallops were cooked.
4. Mix salt, pepper, chicken broth and flour until smooth and add to scallion mixture.
5. Cook macaroni according to directions on package; drain. Place in serving dish and mix with sauce. Arrange scallops on top. Serve with Parmesan cheese.

Serves 4.

SHRIMP AND MACARONI CASSEROLE

3 cups Maruzzelle (medium shells)
2 cups cooked shrimp
1 cup diced celery
1 cup grated cheese
2 slightly beaten eggs

2 cups milk
½ teaspoon salt
Dash of pepper
1 tablespoon butter

1. Preheat oven to 350 degrees.
2. Cook Maruzzelle according to directions on package; drain. Place ⅓ in bottom of a 2 quart greased casserole.
3. Add a layer of shrimp (using 1 cup). Cover with ½ cup diced celery. Add ⅓ Maruzzelle. Sprinkle with 2 tablespoons of the grated cheese. Add 1 more cup of shrimp, ½ cup of celery and 2 tablespoons more cheese. Finish with layer of Maruzzelle. Sprinkle the remaining cheese.
4. Combine eggs, milk and seasoning. Pour over Maruzzelle. Dot the top of the casserole with butter. Set casserole in pan of hot water. Bake until firm — about one hour.

Serves 4–6.

SPAGHETTI WITH SHRIMP MARINARA

1 to 1½ pounds raw shrimp,
   shelled and deveined
3 tablespoons oil
2 cloves garlic, chopped
¼ teaspoon oregano

1 (15½ ounce) jar Marinara sauce
Salt to taste
Pinch of red cayenne pepper (optional)
1 pound spaghetti
Grated cheese

1. Cut up shrimp. Heat oil and lightly sauté garlic and oregano; add shrimp and stirring constantly, sauté until almost tender (3–4 minutes).
2. Stir in Marinara sauce, season to taste. Add salt and red pepper. Simmer for about 5 minutes.
3. Meanwhile, cook spaghetti, following package directions; drain. Pour sauce over shrimp reserving a few pieces. Toss and top with reserved shrimp. Serve with grated cheese.

Serves 4–6.

SEAFOOD TETRAZZINI

8 ounces spaghetti
1 cup tomato juice
1 pound raw shrimp
1 pound scallops
1 teaspoon salt
1 teaspoon caraway seeds

2 bay leaves
2 tablespoons butter
2 tablespoons flour
2 cups milk
2 tablespoons dry sherry
¼ cup grated Parmesan cheese

1. Preheat oven to 350 degrees.
2. Cook spaghetti according to package directions; rinse and drain. Toss spaghetti with tomato juice and set aside.
3. Meanwhile, peel and clean shrimp; place in a saucepan with scallops, cover with water. Add salt, caraway seeds and bay leaves. Bring to a boil; then lower heat and simmer for 10 minutes, or until done. Drain.
4. In a saucepan, melt butter; add flour and stir until smooth. Remove from heat and gradually add milk, stirring until smooth. Return to heat and cook, stirring constantly, until thickened. Add sherry and 2 tablespoons of the grated cheese. Add cooked fish to sauce. Add cooked spaghetti in tomato juice, mixing well. Pour into a buttered 2-quart baking dish; sprinkle with remaining grated cheese. Bake for 20 minutes, or until heated through.

Makes 6 servings.

SHRIMP ROLLS WITH CANNELLONI

16 pieces Cannelloni
1 cup shrimp
1 beaten egg

2 tablespoons diced onion
2 tablespoons diced celery
2 tablespoons vegetable or olive oil

1. Cook Cannelloni according to directions on package; drain. Spread on paper towel.
2. Clean and chop shrimp. Mix well with ½ of the beaten egg.
3. Sauté onion and celery in vegetable oil and add to shrimp.
4. Stuff Cannelloni with mixture. Dip in other ½ of beaten egg. Sauté in frying pan in a small amount of oil.

Serves 4.

SHRIMP TOMATO SAUCE WITH LINGUINE

¼ cup diced onion
½ clove finely diced garlic
¼ cup olive oil
3½ cups Italian style peeled tomatoes
1½ teaspoons salt

¼ teaspoon pepper
1 pound raw shrimp
⅓ cup tomato paste
1 pound Linguine

1. Sauté onion and garlic in olive oil.
2. Add tomatoes, salt and pepper and simmer 40 minutes uncovered.
3. Clean shrimp. Add with tomato paste and simmer 5 minutes more.
4. Cook Linguine according to directions on package; drain. Place in serving dish. Pour sauce over Linguine. Arrange shrimp on top.

Serves 4–6.

VERMICELLI PIZZAIOLA WITH SHRIMP

2 cloves garlic, minced
¼ cup olive oil
1 teaspoon oregano
2 tablespoons chopped parsley
Pinch of red pepper seeds (black pepper
   may be substituted)

1 (16-ounce) can tomatoes
Salt to taste
½ pound cleaned and deveined
  · fresh shrimp
1 pound Vermicelli
Grated Parmesan cheese

1. In a skillet brown (do not burn) garlic in olive oil. Add oregano, chopped parsley, pinch of red pepper seeds, and tomatoes, cut up in slivers. Add salt to taste and simmer gently uncovered for 5 minutes. Add ½ pound cleaned and deveined fresh shrimp and cook in sauce for about 10 minutes, or until shrimp are cooked.
2. Cook Vermicelli according to directions on package; drain. Turn onto serving dish and cover with shrimp sauce. Serve with grated cheese if desired.

Serves 4–6.

Note: for a delicious quick substitute use 1 (16 ounce) jar prepared marinara sauce diluted with ½ cup water; bring to boil. Add shrimp, lower heat and simmer 10 minutes or until shrimp are cooked.

TUNA AND DRIED MUSHROOMS WITH SPAGHETTI

½ ounce dried mushrooms
6 large ripe tomatoes
1 clove garlic
¼ cup olive oil
1 cup canned tuna (the Italian kind,
   packed in olive oil)

a handful of chopped parsley
Salt and black pepper to taste
2 tablespoons butter
1 pound spaghetti

1. Soak the dried mushrooms in cold water for half an hour; drain and cut up small. Cut the tomatoes into chunks.
2. Sauté a crushed garlic clove in olive oil until golden, then remove the garlic. Then add the presoaked, dried mushrooms and the tomatoes. Cover and simmer slowly, until the tomatoes are cooked into a purée and the mushrooms are soft. (30 minutes to an hour.)
3. Drain the canned tuna and add it to the sauce. Simmer but do not boil, and do not break it up too much: the tuna should stay in bite size pieces. Add a handful of chopped parsley, salt (if needed) and black pepper. Just before removing from the heat, stir in some butter (in small bits), and serve over hot, drained spaghetti.

Serves 4–6.

TUNA SAUCE FOR MOSTACCIOLI RIGATI

1 onion, sliced
½ cup finely shredded carrot
2 tablespoons chopped pitted ripe olives
1 tablespoon drained capers
1 clove minced garlic
2 tablespoons olive oil
1 (1 pound) can tomato purée

1 (6½ ounce) can chunk-style tuna,
   drained and flaked
¼ teaspoon crushed thyme
¼ teaspoon salt
Dash pepper
8 ounces Mostaccioli Rigati
Grated Parmesan cheese

1. Cook onion, carrot, olives, capers and garlic in oil until onion is tender. Stir in purée, tuna and seasonings. Cover and simmer 10 minutes. Uncover and simmer 5 minutes, stirring occasionally.
2. Cook Mostaccioli as directed on package; drain. Serve sauce over cooked Mostaccioli and sprinkle with grated Parmesan cheese.

Serves 4.

SOLE WITH SPAGHETTI

2 tablespoons butter or margarine
¾ cup chopped onion
1 package (16 ounces) frozen sole fillets,
   thawed and drained or 1 pound fresh
   sole fillets

Salt and pepper to taste
½ cup shredded Cheddar cheese
1 large tomato, cut into wedges
8 ounces spaghetti
2 tablespoons chopped parsley

1. In a small saucepan, melt 1 tablespoon of the butter. Add onion; sauté over medium heat, stirring occasionally, until onion is tender, about 5 minutes.
2. Preheat oven to 425 degrees.
3. Lightly sprinkle one side of each fillet with salt and pepper. Cut fillets in half lengthwise. Spread 2 teaspoons sauteed onion and about 1 tablespoon cheese on each fillet half. Reserve the remaining onion and cheese. Roll up fillets; fasten each with a toothpick. Place in a lightly buttered 9-inch pie plate; dot fillets with remaining butter. Bake, uncovered, for 15 minutes. Remove from oven. Sprinkle the remaining cheese on top of fillets. Add tomato wedges and bake 5 more minutes, or until fish flakes easily when tested with a fork.
4. Meanwhile, cook spaghetti according to directions on package; drain.
5. Toss together cooked spaghetti, remaining reserved onion and parsley. Serve spaghetti with fish and tomato wedges.

Serves 4.

PASTINA WITH ZUCCHINI AND CLAMS

6 large clams	Spray of parsley
1 pint water	1 thin slice garlic
½ teaspoon salt	2 cups sliced zucchini
Dash pepper	½ cup Pastina

1. Wash clams carefully. Place in saucepan with water. Heat until clams open up.
2. Strain clam water through fine sieve and add enough water to make 1 pint. Place in saucepan with salt, pepper, parsley and garlic. Bring to a boil. Add zucchini. Simmer 2 minutes. Add Pastina and simmer until tender, about 8 minutes.
3. Remove clams from shells and chop very fine. Stir lightly into Pastina mixture and serve immediately.

Serves 4.

TUNAFISH CASSEROLE

2 cups medium noodles	¼ cup onions, minced
2 (7 ounce) cans tuna flakes	Salt and pepper to taste
2 eggs, well beaten	1 can mushroom soup
½ cup breadcrumbs	Dash Worcestershire sauce
½ cup mayonnaise	Dash curry powder

Sauce:

½ cup mayonnaise	½ cup grated cucumber
½ cup sour cream or yoghurt	Salt and pepper to taste

1. Preheat oven to 350 degrees.
2. Cook noodles according to directions on package; drain.
3. Blend well tunafish, eggs, breadcrumbs, mayonnaise, onions, salt and pepper, mushroom soup, Worcestershire sauce and curry powder.
4. Place in a greased 5 cup mold and bake 50 minutes in the oven.
5. Meanwhile, prepare sauce by combining mayonnaise, sour cream or yoghurt, grated cucumber and salt and pepper to taste. Refrigerate and serve over the casserole.

Serves 4–6.

SHRIMP SAUCE WITH SPAGHETTI

1½ pounds raw shrimp and 4 tablespoons
   butter (or 1 pound cooked shrimp)
¼ pound butter
1 clove garlic
½ cup olive oil

½ cup tomato sauce
1 pound spaghetti
Salt and pepper to taste
a handful of minced parsley

1. Shell and clean raw shrimp and cook in 4 tablespoons gently foaming butter in a saucepan for 4 or 5 minutes until pink. Take off the heat, chop and reserve in a bowl. (Ready-cooked shrimp can be substituted although it will not taste as good).
2. Crush garlic and put into the same saucepan in which shrimp were cooked. Add more butter and olive oil and cook gently until the garlic is soft. Stir in tomato sauce and the chopped shrimp and heat until very hot but do not boil.
3. Meanwhile, cook spaghetti according to directions on package; drain.
4. Add salt and pepper to sauce, throw on a handful of minced parsley and serve over hot, drained spaghetti.

Serves 4.

TUNA LASAGNE

1 (28 ounce) can tomatoes
1 (8 ounce) can tomato sauce
1 teaspoon oregano
1 teaspoon sugar
½ teaspon powdered garlic
2 (7-ounce) cans tuna, drained

8 ounces Lasagne
1½ cups cottage cheese
1 egg
2 cups shredded Mozzarella cheese
¼ cup grated Parmesan cheese

1. Preheat oven to 350 degrees.
2. In a 2-quart saucepan, combine tomatoes, tomato sauce, oregano, sugar and garlic. Simmer, uncovered, for 30 minutes, stirring occasionally. Add tuna.
2. Cook Lasagne in boiling water until limp, about half-done; drain.
3. Spoon some sauce in a thin layer over the bottom of a flat 2-quart baking dish. Cover with a layer of Lasagne; add another layer of sauce. Beat cottage cheese and egg together; spread half the mixture over the sauce and top with half the Mozzarella cheese. Repeat layers, ending with tuna sauce. Sprinkle Parmesan cheese over top. Bake for 30 minutes. Remove from oven; let stand 15 minutes before cutting into squares for serving.

Serves 6–8.

MEATLESS

MAIN DISHES

Classic Pesto Genovese with Linguine and a green salad adds elegance to any dinner. With the rising cost of meat try broccoli and Pasta or Ziti with Zucchini for a pleasant main meatless course. One or two meatless macaroni casseroles on a buffet table will add spice to your next large dinner party.

FETTUCCINE ALFREDO

1 pound Fettuccine
8 tablespoons butter (¼ pound)
¼ cup heavy cream
½ cup freshly grated Parmesan cheese

Salt and pepper to taste
1 canned white truffle,
    finely chopped (optional)

1. Cook Fettuccine according to directions on package; drain.
2. Cream the ¼ pound butter until fluffy. Beat in cream a little at a time. Then gradually add grated cheese.
3. Meanwhile, transfer hot cooked Fettuccine to a hot serving bowl. Add the creamed butter and cheese mixture and toss it until every strand is coated. Taste and season generously with salt and pepper. Stir in truffle if used. Serve at once, with a little extra cheese in a separate bowl.

Serves 4–6.

ASPARAGUS-MACARONI CASSEROLE

8 ounces elbow macaroni
1 pound fresh asparagus or 1 package
    frozen asparagus spears
½ cup slivered almonds
1 (10½ ounce) can condensed cream of
    mushroom soup

1 cup milk
2 tablespoons chopped chives
¾ teaspoon salt
Dash of pepper
1½ cups grated Cheddar cheese
3 hard-cooked eggs, sliced

1. Preheat oven to 350 degrees.
2. Cook elbow macaroni according to directions on package; drain.
3. Cook asparagus until just tender; drain and cut into ½ inch pieces.
4. In a shallow pan toast almonds in oven for about 5 minutes.
5. In a large bowl, gradually add milk to mushroom soup; add chives, salt, pepper, 1 cup of the Cheddar cheese, sliced eggs, macaroni, asparagus and almonds. Turn into a buttered 2-quart casserole. Bake in oven 40 minutes; sprinkle remaining Cheddar cheese on top and return to oven for 5 minutes, or until cheese is melted.

Makes 8 servings.

SPAGHETTI WITH ARTICHOKE SAUCE

1 pint water
Juice of ½ lemon
2–3 medium artichokes
⅛ pound salt pork
2 tablespoons olive oil
½ clove minced garlic
½ cup dry white wine

⅓ cup chopped parsley
¼ teaspoon dried basil
1¾ cups canned plum tomatoes
Salt and pepper to taste
1 pound spaghetti
Grated Parmesan cheese

1. Combine water and lemon juice in a deep bowl.
2. Discard the tough outer leaves of the artichokes, cut down the stems to about ½ inch from the base. Cut off the tough points of the leaves, leaving the leaves about 2½ inches long. Cut the artichokes into quarters (as if they were apples) and drop immediately into the lemon-water. Take each piece at a time and cut out the fuzzy choke (as if coring an apple), then cut down into thin slices (lengthwise) and return to the water.
3. Soak the salt pork in cold water for 5 minutes to remove the salt, then dry with paper towels, and chop fine.
4. Heat the olive oil in a saucepan, add the minced salt pork and cook gently for a few minutes.
5. Meanwhile, drain the artichoke slices and pat dry, then add them to the saucepan along with the minced garlic. Continue sautéeing gently over a low fire, stirring frequently, until the artichokes are half tender (5 minutes or so.)
6. Add the white wine, parsley, basil, the tomatoes, salt and pepper to taste. Simmer, covered, for another 20 minutes or so, stirring occasionally, until the artichokes are very tender.
7. Meanwhile, cook the spaghetti according to the directions on the package; drain. Serve the sauce over the hot spaghetti. Sprinkle with Parmesan cheese on the table.

Serves 4–6.

FETTUCCINE WITH ANCHOVY BUTTER
"Alla Romana"

¼ pound butter
8 tablespoons (4 ounces) anchovy paste

½ pound Fettuccine
Grated Parmesan cheese

1. Cream the butter and anchovy paste together with a wooden spoon or food processor until smoothly blended.
2. Meanwhile, cook the Fettuccine according to the directions on the package; drain. Serve the anchovy butter with the Fettuccine. Sprinkle with grated Parmesan cheese.
Serves 2-4.

BROCCOLI-NOODLE CASSEROLE

8 ounces wide noodles
2 (10 ounce) packages frozen
   chopped broccoli, cooked
½ cup shredded Cheddar cheese
2 tablespoons butter

1 tablespoon flour
¾ cup heavy sweet cream
½ teaspoon salt
½ teaspoon Worcestershire sauce

1. Preheat oven to 350 degrees.
2. Cook noodles according to directions on package; drain.
3. Combine cooked noodles and broccoli (reserve liquid from broccoli). Add Cheddar cheese; mix thoroughly.
4. In a small saucepan, melt butter; add flour and stir until thickened. Remove from heat; gradually add cream. Return to heat; cook and stir until sauce is thickened. Add salt, Worcestershire sauce and ¼ cup of the reserved broccoli liquid; cook and stir a minute more. Pour sauce over broccoli mixture and mix thoroughly. Turn into a buttered 1½ quart casserole. Bake in oven for 30 minutes.
Makes 6 servings.

RICH MASCARPONE SAUCE WITH EGG NOODLES

½ pound egg noodles
1 cup (½ pound butter)
½ pound Italian Mascarpone (or other
   rich triple-creme cheese like
   French Fontainebleau or a rich cottage
   cheese mixed with 2 tablespoons of
   heavy sweet cream and sieved)

1. Cook egg noodles according to the directions on the package; drain.
2. Immediately melt the butter and Mascarpone cheese (or substitute over the hot egg noodles). Mix until all the cheese melts.

Serves 4.

ZITI AL FORNO
(Cheese Baked Macaroni)

4 tablespoons butter
4 tablespoons flour
3 cups milk
1 cup diced Mozzarella cheese
½ cup grated Parmesan cheese
½ cup grated cheddar cheese
1 tablespoon grated onion

1 tablespoon steak sauce
1 teaspoon salt
Freshly ground black pepper
8 ounces Ziti macaroni
4 medium sliced tomatoes
Additional grated Parmesan cheese

1. Preheat oven to 325 degrees.
2. Melt butter, add flour and blend until smooth. Add milk and cook until thickened, stirring constantly. Add cheeses, onion, steak sauce, salt and pepper. Cook until cheese melts, stirring constantly, then remove from heat.
3. Cook Ziti according to package directions; drain. Add to cheese mixture. Put half of this mixture into a greased 2 quart casserole and arrange half of the tomato slices on top. Repeat. Sprinkle with additional grated cheese if desired.
4. Bake in oven for 20 minutes. Broil under medium heat for about 10 minutes or until cheese sauce bubbles and begins to brown.
Serves 4-6.

VERMICELLI WITH LEMON-MUSHROOM SAUCE

½ pound sliced fresh mushrooms
¼ cup sliced scallions
¼ cup butter
¼ cup lemon juice

½ teaspoon salt
¼ teaspoon pepper
8 ounces Vermicelli

1. Cook mushrooms and scallions in butter until onions are tender. Stir in lemon juice and salt and pepper. Heat thoroughly.
2. Cook Vermicelli as directed on package; drain. Serve sauce over cooked Vermicelli.
Serves 4.

SHELL AND CHEESE PUFF

6 tablespoons butter or margarine
¼ cup flour
1½ teaspoons salt
1½ teaspoons dry mustard
½ teaspoon paprika
2 cups milk

½ pound Cheddar cheese, shredded
 (2 cups)
6 eggs, separated
8 ounces Maruzzelle shells
Sesame seeds

1. Preheat oven to 350 degrees.
2. Melt butter in a saucepan and blend in flour, salt, mustard and paprika. Cook, stirring constantly. Add milk, and continue stirring until sauce thickens. Add cheese, stir until it melts, and remove from heat.
3. Beat egg whites until they form soft peaks.
4. In a separate bowl, beat egg yolks until creamy and thick. Gradually add cooked cheese sauce, stirring until well-blended.
5. Meanwhile, cook Maruzzelle according to directions on package; drain. Add Maruzzelle to the above and lightly stir in egg whites. Pour into an ungreased 8 cup soufflé dish.
6. To give a tiered top, gently cut a deep circle in the mixture about an inch in from the outside edge. Sprinkle with sesame seeds and bake for 1 hour or until puffed and golden brown.
Serves 6-8.

STUFFED GREEN PEPPERS

1 cup Tubettini
4 green peppers
2 tablespoons flour
2 tablespoons butter or margarine
1 cup milk

½ cup diced American cheese
½ teaspoon salt
Dash of pepper
½ teaspoon horseradish
Paprika

1. Preheat oven to 375 degrees.
2. Cook Tubettini according to directions on package; drain.
3. Cut tops from green peppers; remove seeds and pith. Parboil 5 minutes.
4. Prepare a white sauce by combining flour and butter over low heat in a saucepan. Add milk gradually, stirring constantly until thickened.
5. Add cheese, salt and pepper, and horseradish to sauce, stirring until smooth. Add Tubettini. Fill peppers with Tubettini mixture. Place in shallow baking pan with ¼ inch of water.
6. Sprinkle paprika on top. Bake in oven 35-40 minutes.

Serves 4.

MEZZANI SICILIANA
(Baked Macaroni and Eggplant — Sicilian Style)

1 medium eggplant
½ cup olive oil
1 clove chopped garlic
1 #2 ½ can (3 cups) Italian style
   peeled tomatoes

1 basil leaf
½ teaspoon salt
Dash of pepper
1 pound Mezzani
Grated Parmesan cheese

1. Preheat oven to 350 degrees.
2. Skin and slice eggplant thin. Fry in oil in a large frying pan until brown. Remove slices. Set aside on paper towel or brown paper.
3. Add garlic, tomatoes, basil, salt and pepper to remaining oil in frying pan. Simmer for 15 minutes, stirring frequently with a fork.
4. Cook Mezzani according to package instructions; drain.
5. In a greased casserole place a layer of Mezzani (using ⅓ of Mezzani); then a layer of eggplant slices (using ½ eggplant.) Sprinkle with Parmesan cheese. Repeat, ending with a layer of Mezzani. Pour sauce over Mezzani. Bake in oven 10-15 minutes.

Serves 6.

SPAGHETTI WITH "PEPERONATA"
(Sweet Pepper Sauce)

1 onion	6 tomatoes
3 tablespoons olive oil	Salt and pepper to taste
2 tablespoons butter	12 ounces spaghetti
4 large sweet bell peppers	Grated Parmesan cheese

1. Slice onion fine and sauté in olive oil and butter. When golden, add sweet bell peppers, peeled, seeded and sliced. (See note.) Sauté until nicely colored, then add tomatoes, peeled and chopped small. Add salt and pepper and simmer until tomaotes cook down to a good consistency and the peppers are soft. Thin with a little boiling water, if necessary.
2. Cook spaghetti according to the directions on the package; drain and serve covered with the pepper sauce. Add grated Parmesan cheese on the table.

Serves 4.

Note: This tastes best when the peppers have been singed and peeled. Hold over the flame with a long-handled fork, turn, and singe all over or put in a 450 degrees oven for 20 minutes. This makes the skin slip off easily, and also gives a delicious charred flavor.

GARDEN CASSEROLE

1 cup Ditalini	4 tablespoons butter or margarine
½ cup green peas	2 cups milk
1 cup diced carrots	1 teaspoon salt
½ cup diced celery	Dash of pepper
1 cup fresh string beans	½ cup buttered breadcrumbs*
4 tablespoons flour	

1. Preheat oven to 400 degrees.
2. Cook Ditalini according to directions on package; drain.
3. Cook peas, carrots, celery and string beans in salted boiling water until they are just done.
4. Combine flour and butter over low heat. Add milk gradually, stirring until it thickens. Season with salt and pepper.
5. Combine Ditalini, vegetables and sauce. Pour into a greased 1½ quart casserole.
6. Sprinkle breadcrumbs on top. Bake for 30 minutes or until crumbs are brown.

Serves 4-6.

*Buttered Breadcrumbs: Mix ½ cup fine dry breadcrumbs with 2 tablespoons butter or margarine, melted.

NOODLE SPINACH RING

1 (8 ounce) package broad noodles
2 (10 ounce) packages chopped,
  defrosted spinach, drained
½ cup butter

1 onion
3 eggs, slightly beaten
1 cup sour cream
1 pound steamed mushrooms

1. Preheat oven to 350 degrees.
2. Cook noodles in salted water until barely tender and drain; mix noodles and spinach.
3. Sauté onion in butter until slightly browned. Fold in eggs; add sour cream and blend well.
   Pour into a greased 6 cup ring mold. Place mold in pan of hot water in oven for 45 minutes.
   Unmold. Serve on heated platter with steamed mushrooms in the center.
Serves 8.

QUICK 'N' EASY MANICOTTI

1 pound Ricotta cheese
4 ounces skim milk Mozzarella cheese,
  grated
3 tablespoons grated Parmesan cheese
2 teaspoons sugar
1 slightly beaten egg

1 tablespoon finely chopped parsley
Salt and pepper to taste
1 (5 ounce) package Manicotti
2 (15½ ounces) jars prepared meatless
  or Marinara sauce

1. Preheat oven to 400 degrees.
2. Mix and blend well Ricotta, Mozzarella, grated Parmesan cheese, sugar, egg, parsley, salt
   and pepper to taste.
3. Stuff uncooked Manicotti generously with cheese mixture from both ends. Arrange
   stuffed Manicotti in a single layer in a baking pan. Bring sauce to a boil and pour over
   Manicotti to completely cover. Cover baking pan with aluminum foil, crimping edges to
   seal tightly.
4. Bake in oven for 40 minutes. Remove foil, sprinkle generously with additional grated
   cheese, and bake, uncovered, for 5 minutes longer.
Serves 6.
Note: See page 132 for more elaborate version.

BAKED SPAGHETTI WITH PARSLEY

5 tablespoons butter or margarine
1 cup finely chopped parsley
3 tablespoons all-purpose flour
1¼ teaspoons salt
Dash of pepper
3 cups milk

2 tablespoons undrained horseradish
2 teaspoons prepared mustard
½ pound spaghetti
3 cups grated Cheddar cheese
Chopped parsley for garnish, optional

1. Preheat oven to 400 degrees.
2. In a large saucepan, melt 2 tablespoons of the butter. Add parsley; sauté over medium heat, stirring constantly until parsley is tender, about 2 minutes. Remove parsley; set aside.
3. In same saucepan, melt remaining 3 tablespoons butter; blend in flour, salt and pepper. Cook over low heat, stirring constantly, until mixture is smooth and bubbly. Gradually stir in milk, horseradish and mustard; cook, stirring constantly, until mixture thickens and begins to boil. Remove from heat.
4. Cook spaghetti according to directions on package; drain.
5. Reserve ½ cup cheese; add remaining cheese to sauce and stir until cheese is melted. Stir in spaghetti and parsley until combined. Pour into an ungreased 2-quart casserole. Sprinkle top with reserved cheese. Bake for 20 minutes or until hot and bubbly. Sprinkle with chopped parsley if desired. Serve immediately.

Serves 4-6.

PESTO GENOVESE WITH VERMICELLI

⅓ cup olive oil
1 cup fresh basil leaves
6 cloves garlic (or to taste)
½ cup grated Parmesan cheese
¼ cup pine nuts or coarsely
    chopped walnuts

1 tablespoon butter
½ teaspoon salt
Dash of pepper
½ pound Vermicelli

1. In an electric blender or food processor, combine oil, basil, garlic, cheese, nuts, butter, salt and pepper. Blend at high speed to a pastelike consistency, about 1 minute. *Or,* to make by hand, crush basil with a mortar and pestle until pastelike. Work in salt and pepper, garlic, nuts, butter and then add olive oil a little at a time. Lastly, mix in the grated cheese.
2. Cook Vermicelli according to directions on the package; drain. Toss Pesto together with the hot Vermicelli and serve immediately.

Serves 4.

Note: Fresh basil is essential for this deliciously crunchy recipe. Pesto freezes well and can last throughout the winter. Add a dollop to your favorite soup for flavor.

MACARONI SPINACH CASSEROLE

1 pound elbow macaroni
1 medium chopped onion
½ cup butter or margarine
½ cup flour
2½ teaspoons salt
5 cups milk

2 beaten eggs
1 cup creamed cottage cheese
2 (10 ounce) packages frozen chopped
    spinach, cooked and drained
Buttered breadcrumbs*

1. Preheat oven to 350 degrees.
2. Cook elbow macaroni according to directions on package; drain.
3. In medium saucepan, sauté onion in butter until crisp. Blend in flour and salt.
4. Gradually add 4 cups of the milk. Cook, stirring constantly, until sauce boils 2 minutes. Blend remaining milk and eggs; stir into sauce with cheese.
5. Place half the macaroni in a shallow 3-quart casserole. Top with spinach, ½ the sauce and then the remaining macaroni. Pour remaining sauce on top and sprinkle with buttered breadcrumbs. Bake 20 minutes.

Makes 8 servings.

*Buttered Breadcrumbs: Mix ½ cup fine dry breadcrumbs with 2 tablespoons butter or margarine, melted.

MARUZZE IN WHITE WINE

1 pound Maruzze shells
⅓ cup half and half
⅓ cup white wine
2 cans Cheddar cheese soup

2 tablespoons tarragon
1 tablespoon chopped parsley
Paprika

1. Preheat oven to 325 degrees.
2. Cook Maruzze shells according to directions on package; drain and put them in a buttered casserole dish.
3. Combine half and half, white wine, cheddar cheese soup and tarragon in a mixing bowl and when well stirred, pour over the shells.
4. Sprinkle a little chopped parsley and paprika on top for color and bake, covered for 20 minutes. Uncover casserole and bake another 5 or 10 minutes.

Serves 4-6.

LINGUINE A LA MARINARA*

½ cup olive oil
2 cloves minced garlic
1 #2 ½ can tomatoes
¼ teaspoon oregano
Salt and pepper to taste

¼ teaspoon dried basil
½ teaspoon thyme
1 pound Linguine
2 tablespoons chopped parsley

1. Simmer garlic in oil in frying pan until light brown.
2. Add tomatoes, oregano, salt and pepper and basil; mash and stir constantly with a fork 5 minutes. Sprinkle with thyme and stir.
3. Cook Linguine according to directions on package and drain well. Add sauce. Sprinkle with parsley and serve.

Serves 4-6.

*"Marinara" means "sailor-style" in a spicy, meatless sauce.

LINGUINE TERRA JOYA
(Linguine with Artichokes in White Sauce)

Sauce:

¼ cup olive oil
½ stick (¼ cup) butter or margarine
1 teaspoon flour
1 cup chicken stock or broth
1 garlic clove, crushed
2 teaspoons lemon juice

1 teaspoon minced flat-leafed parsley
Salt and pepper to taste
8 artichoke hearts, cooked and drained
4 tablespoons freshly grated
  Parmesan cheese
2 teaspoons drained capers

1. Heat olive oil in a large heavy skillet over moderately low heat; add butter or margarine, melt it and add flour. Cook the mixture, stirring, for 3 minutes.
2. Stir in 1 cup chicken stock or broth, heated. Turn heat up to moderately high, and cook the sauce for 1 minute.
3. Add garlic clove, lemon juice, parsley, salt and pepper and cook sauce over moderately low heat, stirring occasionally, for 5 minutes.
3. Add artichoke hearts, Parmesan cheese, capers, and cook covered, basting the artichoke hearts with the sauce several times, for 8 minutes.

Linguine:

1 pound Linguine
2 tablespoons olive oil
1 tablespoon freshly grated
  Parmesan cheese

1 tablespoon softened butter
¼ teaspoon salt
¼ cup minced proscuitto

1. Cook 1 pound Linguine in 6 quarts boiling salted water for 10 minutes, or until it is just tender, and drain.
2. In the kettle in which the Linguine was cooked, combine 2 tablespoons olive oil, 1 tablespoon each of freshly grated Parmesan cheese and softened butter, and ¼ teaspoon salt.
3. Return the drained Linguine to the kettle and toss it with the cheese mixture.
4. Divide the pasta among 4 heated bowls, top it with sauce and garnish each serving with 1 tablespoon minced proscuitto. Serve additional grated Parmesan cheese separately.
Serves 4.

PASTA

SIDE DISHES

Buttered noodles with poppy seeds, cheese macaroni or spaghetti with tomato sauce are delicious accompaniments to your favorite steak, roast or fish dish.

PARSLIED PASTINA

1 cup Pastina
¼ cup butter or olive oil

½ teaspoon white pepper
1 cup chopped parsley

1. Cook Pastina as directed on package; drain.
2. Melt butter in frying pan. Add pepper and Pastina. Heat thoroughly, stirring lightly. Stir in parsley and serve immediately as a vegetable with poultry or fish.
Serves 4.

PASTINA CORN PUDDING

2 cups milk
½ cup Pastina
¼ cup diced onion
2 tablespoons vegetable oil
2 eggs

2 cups whole kernel corn
2 teaspoons salt
1 teaspoon celery salt
Dash of white pepper

1. Preheat oven to 325 degrees.
2. Heat milk in top of double boiler. Add Pastina and cook 15 minutes, stirring frequently for the first 5 minutes.
3. Sauté onion in oil for 5 minutes or until tender. Beat eggs thoroughly. Combine with corn, Pastina, onions and seasonings. Blend thoroughly. Turn into greased deep 8-inch cake pan. Bake in oven for 45 minutes or until firm.
Serves 4-6.

PASTINA CHILI

1 cup Pastina
1 clove garlic
3 tablespoons oil

1 (8 ounce) can (¾ cup) prepared
   tomato sauce
1 teaspoon chili powder

1. Cook Pastina as directed on package; drain.
2. Chop garlic very fine and saute in fat over low heat for 1 minute. Add tomato sauce and chili powder. Simmer uncovered 5 minutes. Add Pastina. Heat thoroughly and serve immediately with meatballs, sausage or lamb.

Serves 4.

CARROT AND PASTINA MOLD

3 tablespoons butter
3 tablespoons flour
1 cup milk
1 teaspoon salt
Dash white pepper

¼ teaspoon celery salt
¼ teaspoon onion salt
2 eggs
½ cup Pastina
2 cups finely shredded carrots

1. Make a white sauce by melting the butter in a saucepan over moderate heat without letting it brown. Add the flour and stir until well blended. Heat the milk almost to boiling and stir into the flour-butter roux all at once. When the mixture comes to a boil it will thicken automatically. Simmer for a few minutes. Add salt, pepper, celery and onion salt. Remove from heat. Cool slightly.
2. Beat eggs thoroughly. Stir in a little of the white sauce. Then blend eggs into sauce gradually.
3. Cook Pastina as directed on package; drain.
4. Cook carrots in tightly covered saucepan in boiling salted water until tender crisp, about 8 minutes. Lightly stir Pastina and carrots into sauce. Pour into greased 1-quart ring mold. Bake in oven for 30 minutes or until firm. Turn out on hot platter and fill center with green peas or asparagus tips. Garnish with parsley or watercress.

Serves 4–6.

SHELL MACARONI WITH TOMATO MUSHROOM SAUCE

¼ cup finely chopped onion
¼ cup chopped green pepper
¼ cup olive oil
1 pound sliced mushrooms

1 can (1¼ cups) condensed undiluted
    tomato soup
2½ cups shells

1. Sauté onions and green pepper in oil. Add mushrooms. Cover and cook over moderate heat for 5 minutes. Add tomato soup and bring to a boil.
2. Cook shells according to directions on package; drain. Place in serving dish. Pour sauce over shells. Toss lightly.

Serves 4.

ELBOW MACARONI WITH WINE CHEESE SAUCE

2 cups elbow macaroni
½ cup diced onion
2 tablespoons diced green peppers
2 tablespoons vegetable oil
1 cup tomato juice

½ teaspoon salt
Dash of pepper
½ pound diced processed American
    cheese
½ cup sherry

1. Cook elbows according to directions on the package; drain.
2. Sauté onion and green pepper in vegetable oil.
3. Add tomato juice, salt, pepper, American cheese and sherry. Cook over low heat until cheese melts. Place elbows in serving dish. Pour sauce over it. Toss lightly.

Serves 4.

EGG BOWS WITH FRESH MUSHROOM SAUCE

¼ cup chopped onion
½ clove finely chopped garlic
½ cup vegetable oil
1 pound fresh mushrooms sliced

1 cup seasoned beef broth
1 tablespoon chopped parsley
2½ cups small egg bows

1. Sauté onion and garlic in oil. Add mushrooms and cook 10 minutes. Add hot beef broth and parsley and continue to cook over moderate heat for 15 minutes more.
2. Cook egg bows according to directions on package; drain. Place in serving dish. Pour sauce over egg bows. Toss lightly.

Serves 4.

NOODLES WITH TOMATO CHEESE SAUCE

½ pound wide egg noodles
¼ cup chopped green pepper
2 tablespoons vegetable oil
1 can (1¼ cups) condensed undiluted
   tomato soup

¼ pound diced American cheese
½ teaspoon Worcestershire sauce

1. Cook noodles according to package directions; drain.
2. Sauté green pepper in oil in sauce pan. Add tomato soup and heat thoroughly. Reduce heat. Add American cheese and Worcestershire sauce and stir until cheese melts. Pour sauce over noodles on serving dish. Toss lightly.

Serves 4.

FRENCH STYLE MACARONI

1 pound elbow macaroni ½ cup butter
1 pint seasoned beef broth ½ cup grated Parmesan cheese

1. Cook elbow macaroni according to directions on package; drain.
2. Heat beef broth and pour over elbow macaroni.
3. Add butter and cheese. Mix all the ingredients well together. Heat over low flame 5 minutes. Serve hot with more grated Parmesan cheese.
Serves 6.

PAN FRIED NOODLES

½ pound fine egg noodles
¼ cup vegetable oil

1. Cook egg noodles according to the directions on the package and drain well. Place on paper towel. Allow to dry thoroughly.
2. Sauté in vegetable oil in a frying pan over moderate heat. Brown on one side. Turn noodles with pancake turner, brown on other side. Place in serving dish.
Serves 4.

DEEP FAT FRIED NOODLES

½ pound fine egg noodles
1 quart vegetable oil or Crisco
Salt to taste

1. Cook egg noodles according to package directions and drain. Place on paper towel. Allow to dry thoroughly.
2. In a deep fat frying pan, heat fat to 390 degrees. Add one half of the cooked dry noodles. Turn off heat while adding noodles. Cook over moderate heat until golden brown. Drain on paper towel. Sprinkle with salt. Cook remaining half of noodles using same directions.
Serves 4.

NOODLES WITH POPPY SEEDS

½ pound medium egg noodles
¼ cup butter
2 teaspoons poppy seeds

1. Cook egg noodles according to the package directions and drain.
2. In a saucepan melt the butter and add the poppy seeds.
   Place noodles in a serving dish. Pour sauce over noodles. Toss lightly and serve as a side dish.
Serves 4.

FIDEOS TOSTADOS (Toasted Fideo)*

1 (12 ounce) package Fideos
½ cup olive oil
2 cups strained stewed tomatoes

3 cups water
1 teaspoon salt or to taste

1. Pan fry the Fideos coils in oil until golden brown. Set aside in another pan.
2. Add the tomatoes, water and salt to the original pan, boil and then add the Fideos. Simmer, semi-covered for about 10 minutes, stirring occasionally with a long fork to separate coils and keep noodles from sticking. Cook until Fideos is tender and liquid is absorbed.
3. Remove from heat and let sit covered about 10 minutes before serving. Stir again. Goes well with Chicken Cacciatore.
Serves 6.
Note: Preparing this dish in advance only improves the taste. Cover to reheat.

*An old Spanish-Jewish recipe.

DITALI WITH OLIVE SAUCE

¼ cup finely chopped onion
4 tablespoons olive oil
2½ cups tomatoes
½ teaspoon salt
Pepper to taste

2 tablespoons tomato paste
1 cup chopped ripe olives
⅓ cup grated Parmesan cheese
2½ cups Ditali

1. Sauté onion in olive oil in saucepan. Add tomatoes and salt and pepper and simmer for 40 minutes uncovered. Add tomato paste, olives and Parmesan cheese and simmer an additional 10 minutes.
2. Cook Ditali according to directions on package; drain. Place in serving dish. Pour sauce over Ditali, tossing lightly.
Serves 4.

SPAGHETTI CON AGLIO E OLIO
(Spaghetti with Garlic and Oil Sauce)

½ cup olive oil
6 cloves finely chopped garlic
½ cup chopped parsley
a good pinch oregano

Salt and pepper to taste
12 ounces spaghetti
Grated Parmesan cheese

1. Heat olive oil, add the chopped garlic and simmer very gently until just golden (2–3 minutes.)
2. Stir in the chopped parsley, a good pinch of oregano, salt and pepper to taste and cook for another few minutes.
3. Meanwhile, cook the spaghetti according to the directions on the package; drain.
4. Serve the sauce over the hot, drained spaghetti. Add grated Parmesan cheese at the table.
Serves 4.

MACARONI SHELLS WITH FRIED ONION SAUCE

1 quart sliced onions
½ cup vegetable or olive oil
½ teaspoon salt

Dash of pepper
2 cups shell macaroni

1. Sauté onions in oil in frying pan. Season with salt and pepper. Cover frying pan and simmer 15 minutes. Uncover and allow onions to brown.
2. Cook shells according to directions on package; drain. Place in serving dish. Pour sauce over shells. Toss lightly.

Serves 4.

ELBOW MACARONI WITH FRESH TOMATO SAUCE

¼ cup finely chopped onion
1 clove finely chopped garlic
¼ cup finely chopped celery
⅓ cup vegetable oil
2 tablespoons chopped parsley

2 chopped basil leaves
1 teaspoon salt
Dash of pepper
8 ripe peeled diced tomatoes (4 cups)
2 cups elbow macaroni

1. Sauté onions, garlic, and celery in oil in saucepan.
2. Add parsley, basil, salt, pepper and tomatoes. Bring to boil and then simmer 40 minutes uncovered until sauce is creamy.
3. Cook elbow macaroni according to the directions on package; drain. Serve with sauce over elbows. Toss lightly.

Serves 4.

RICOTTA CHEESE SAUCE

1 cup (½ pound) Ricotta cheese   12 ounces egg noodles
¼ cup grated Parmesan cheese   ¼ cup butter
Salt and pepper to taste

1. Cream Ricotta cheese with a wooden spoon until smooth, straining if necessary. Blend in grated Parmesan cheese, and salt and pepper to taste.
2. Meanwhile, cook the egg noodles according to the direction on the package; drain. Melt the butter over the hot egg noodles. Add the Ricotta mixture and serve immediately.
Serves 4.

VERMICELLI PANCAKES

5 ounces Vermicelli   Dash of nutmeg
3 eggs   Butter for frying
Salt and pepper to taste

1. Cook Vermicelli according to directions on package; drain, and cut up.
2. Beat eggs until light and combine with the Vermicelli; season to taste with salt and pepper and add nutmeg.
3. Drop by tablespoonfuls in hot butter, spreading slightly with the back of the spoon. Brown the pancakes lightly on both sides. Serve as a side dish with meat, fish or fowl.
Serves 4.

ZITI WITH ZUCCHINI

3–4 medium zucchini
4 tablespoons butter
1 medium onion, minced
Salt and pepper to taste

½ pound Ziti Rigati
2 eggs
¼ cup grated Parmesan cheese

1. Preheat oven to 350 degrees.
2. Wash and scrub zucchini (do not peel), and slice into thin rounds. Sauté in butter with onion until zucchini are tender. Season with salt and pepper to taste.
3. Cook Ziti according to directions on package; drain.
4. Meanwhile, beat eggs with grated cheese and a pinch of pepper. Turn macaroni into a deep serving dish. Pour beaten eggs over them. Toss and mix quickly; fold in cooked zucchini. Sprinkle with additional grated cheese and bake in oven for 20 minutes to brown lightly.

Serves 4–6.

PASTINA VEGETABLE CASSEROLE

½ cup Pastina
¼ cup diced onion
2 tablespoons butter or margarine
1 cup cooked diced carrots
1 cup cooked green peas
1 cup cooked diced celery
6 tablespoons oil

6 tablespoons flour
1 pint milk
2 teaspoons salt
¼ teaspoon white pepper
¼ teaspoon onion salt
½ cup soft breadcrumbs
2 tablespoons butter, melted

1. Preheat oven to 425 degrees.
2. Cook Pastina as directed on package; drain.
3. Sauté onion in butter until tender. Combine with Pastina and vegetables. Place in greased 2 quart casserole.
4. Make a white sauce of the oil, flour, milk and salt, pepper and onion salt.
5. Pour sauce into casserole, stirring gently. Combine breadcrumbs and melted butter. Sprinkle over casserole and bake in oven for 30 minutes or until thoroughly hot and the breadcrumbs are golden brown.

Serves 4–6.

DESSERTS

Noodle Puddings have been Eastern European dessert favorites for centuries. In any county, noodles or Pastina enhance the taste of fruits in a variety of delicious sweet ways from Brown Betty to Egg Custard.

APPLESAUCE NOODLE PUDDING

1 (8 ounce) package wide noodles
½ pound cottage cheese
1 cup sour cream
1 cup applesauce

3 eggs, well beaten
1 teaspoon salt
¼ cup butter

1. Preheat oven to 350 degrees.
2. Cook noodles according to directions on package; drain.
3. Stir cottage cheese, sour cream and applesauce together; add the eggs and salt. Break butter into tiny pieces and add to mixture. Fold in cooked noodles. Pour into a buttered 1 quart casserole and bake for one hour. Raise the heat to 400 degrees the last 15 minutes to brown the pudding.

Serves 6.

APPLE BROWN BETTY

¾ cup shell macaroni
1 quart sliced unpeeled apples
¼ cup butter or margarine
⅓ cup sugar
¼ teaspoon nutmeg

¼ teaspoon cinnamon
1 tablespoon lemon juice
1 tablespoon grated lemon rind
Heavy cream or hard sauce

1. Cook shells according to the directions on the package; drain.
2. Sauté apples in butter or margarine in the frying pan. Cover and cook over moderate heat until apples are tender — about 15 minutes.
3. Add sugar, nutmeg, cinnamon, lemon juice and lemon rind to the shells. Then combine with cooked apples in the frying pan. Stir lightly. Cover and cook 5 minutes. Serve warm with cream or hard sauce.

Serves 6.

EGG NOODLE CUSTARD

4 ounces fine egg noodles
2 eggs, separated
1 cup hot milk
½ cup sugar or honey

¼ teaspoon salt
4 ounces blanched almonds
½ teaspoon vanilla
⅔ cup heavy cream, whipped

1. Preheat the oven to 325 degrees.
2. Cook the noodles according to the directions on the package; drain.
3. Beat the yolks until fluffy. Blend the milk, sugar and salt and pour slowly over the beaten yolks. Cook over hot water, stirring constantly, until mixture coats a spoon. Cook until lukewarm.
4. Mix almonds, vanilla and milk mixture with the noodles.
5. Fold in egg whites which have been beaten stiff, but not dry. Pour in a one quart ring mold buttered on the bottom only. Bake for one hour. Turn out of mold onto serving dish.
Serve with whipped cream. Serves 4–6.

LOKSHEN KUGEL–Noodle Pudding

1 pound broad noodles
1 cup sour cream
1 pound cottage cheese
4 eggs
1 cup milk
1 cup raisins

½ cup sugar
Pinch of salt
1 cup crushed cornflakes
¼ pound melted butter
1 tablespoon cinnamon

1. Cook noodles according to directions on packages; drain and rinse with cold water.
2. Mix noodles with sour cream, cottage cheese, eggs, milk, raisins, sugar and salt.
3. Preheat oven to 375 degrees.
4. Place mixture in a 3 quart baking dish. Top with mixture of crushed cornflakes, melted butter and cinnamon. Refrigerate for 3 hours.
5. Bake in oven for 1¼ hours.
Serves 8–10.

NOODLE FRUIT PUDDING

4 ounces medium egg noodles
1 pound dried prunes

¼ cup butter or margarine
⅓ cup orange marmalade

1. Preheat oven to 350 degrees.
2. Cook egg noodles according to directions on package, and drain.
3. Soak prunes overnight. Drain. Pit and chop. Save 12 prunes for garnish.
4. Melt butter and add to prunes. Add orange marmalade and mix all ingredients with noodles. Pour into a one quart buttered casserole. Garnish top with 12 pitted prunes. Bake for 30 minutes.

Serves 4–6.

ORANGE CREAM CUSTARD

2 ounces fine egg noodles
⅓ cup sugar
3 tablespoons corn starch
¼ teaspoon salt

1 cup orange juice
1 teaspoon grated orange rind
2 eggs, separated
1 cup rich hot milk

1. Cook egg noodles according to the directions on the package and drain.
2. Blend the sugar, corn starch and salt together. Add the orange juice and rind and stir.
3. Beat the yolks well and add. Cook in double boiler until yolks begin to thicken.
4. Add milk. Stir well. Cook 10 minutes, stirring occasionally. Add noodles, stirring thoroughly. Remove from heat and cool to lukewarm. Beat egg whites until stiff (not dry.) Fold in. Pour into individual custard cups.

Serves 4.

RAISIN PUDDING WITH PASTINA

3 cups milk
½ cup Pastina
½ cup seedless raisins
½ teaspoon salt

1 egg
4 tablespoons sugar or honey
½ teaspoon cinnamon

1. Heat milk in the top of a double boiler. Add Pastina, raisins and salt. Cook for 15 minutes, stirring frequently for the first 5 minutes.
2. Beat egg thoroughly with sugar and cinnamon. Stir a little of hot cooked Pastina into egg. Then pour egg into double boiler gradually, stirring constantly. Cook 5 minutes.
    Serves 4–6.

PASTINA GRAHAM CAKE

1 quart milk
½ cup Pastina
4 eggs, separated
2 tablespoons lemon juice
2 teaspoons salt
2 teaspoons grated lemon rind

½ teaspoon vanilla
1½ tablespoons unflavored gelatine
⅓ cup cold water
¼ cup sugar
1 cup finely crushed graham cracker
    crumbs
2 tablespoons butter

1. Heat the milk in the top of a double boiler. Add Pastina and cook for 15 minutes, stirring frequently for the first 5 minutes.
2. Beat together egg yolks, lemon juice, salt and lemon rind. Stir a little of the hot mixture into eggs. Then pour eggs gradually, stirring constantly, into the double boiler. Cook, stirring gently, until mixture thickens, about 2 minutes. Add vanilla. Soften gelatine in water and add to mixture. Remove from heat and cool until mixture begins to thicken.
3. Beat egg whites until stiff but not dry. Beat in sugar gradually to make a meringue. Fold into cooked mixture, gently. Then pour into lightly oiled 9-inch spring form pan.
4. Blend together graham cracker crumbs and melted butter. Sprinkle evenly over surface. Place in refrigerator and chill overnight. Remove outer rim of spring form. Cut cake into individual pieces and serve.
    Serves 8–10.

PASTINA MOLASSES PUDDING

1 pint milk
¼ cup molasses
1 tablespoon butter

½ teaspoon salt
½ teaspoon ginger
½ cup Pastina

1. Preheat oven to 325 degrees.
2. Scald milk. Add molasses, butter, salt and ginger. Add Pastina and pour into a greased 1-quart casserole. Place in oven stirring every 5 minutes for the first 15 minutes. Bake for 1 hour or until firm.

Serves 4.

PASTINA PINEAPPLE CUSTARD

2 cups pineapple juice
⅓ cup Pastina
Dash of salt

2 eggs
2 tablespoons lemon juice
¼ cup sugar

1. Heat pineapple juice in the top of a double boiler. Add Pastina and salt. Cook for 15 minutes, stirring frequently for the first 5 minutes.
2. Separate eggs and beat yolks with lemon juice. Stir some of hot mixture into eggs. Then gradually, pour eggs into double boiler, stirring constantly. Cook 5 minutes, stirring occasionally or until mixture thickens. Cool slightly.
3. Beat egg whites until stiff but not dry. Beat sugar in thoroughly, 1 tablespoon at a time. Fold into cooked mixture, gradually. Place in individual serving dishes or custard cups. Chill before serving.

Serves 4.

RAISIN/CHEESE NOODLE PUDDING

1 (8 ounce) package medium noodles
3 eggs
1 cup cottage cheese
1 cup sour cream
¼ teaspoon salt

½ cup sugar
2 tablespoons lemon juice
½ cup white seedless raisins
⅓ cup butter
¼ cup fine breadcrumbs

1. Preheat oven to 350 degrees.
2. Cook noodles according to direction on package; drain.
3. Beat eggs; add cottage cheese and sour cream. Add salt, sugar, lemon juice and raisins. Fold noodles into this mixture. Put half of the butter into an 8 x 12 inch baking dish; heat in the oven until butter is melted. Pour noodle mixture into prepared baking dish. Dot top with remaining butter and breadcrumbs. Bake for 1 hour.

Makes 6 servings.

PINEAPPLE NOODLE PUDDING

8 ounces broad noodles
3 eggs
½ pound pot cheese
4 tablespoons butter
1 cup sour cream
½ cup sugar
1 (8 ounce) can crushed pineapple
   with juice

1 teaspoon vanilla
½ cup white seedless raisins
1 cup milk
1 tablespoon sugar
1 teaspoon cinnamon

1. Preheat oven to 350 degrees, if cooking immediately.
2. Parboil the noodles; rinse and drain.
3. Combine eggs, pot cheese, butter and sour cream; beat well. Add sugar, pineapple and vanilla; mix well. Add raisins and drained noodles.
4. Pour mixture into a buttered baking dish. Pour milk over all. Refrigerate for several hours if possible, before baking. Then sprinkle top with sugar and cinnamon and bake in oven for 1 hour.

Makes 8 servings.

FOR CROWDS
AND
CROWDED TIMES

Planning to serve a large gathering? There is no food that pleases more people and rescues more food budgets than pasta for fifty or more guests. Here are a few recipes for your next large family or friend get together.

Is it your schedule that's crowded? Speed up your cooking preparation time or slow it down with recipes and cooking tips for slow cooker and microwave pasta cookery you'll find in this chapter.

MEAT BALLS AND MACARONI

8 pounds ground beef
4 teaspoons salt
8 small onions, grated
8 eggs, beaten
½ pound vegetable shortening
1 cup flour

2½ tablespoons chili powder
8 bay leaves
4 (18 ounce) cans tomato juice
5 pounds macaroni
3 cups grated Parmesan cheese

1. Combine beef, salt, onions and eggs and form into meat balls. (Yield 100.) Brown in hot shortening and remove from frying pan.
2. Stir flour into shortening in frying pan. Add chili powder, bay leaves and tomato juice. Cook and stir until thick. Add meat balls to sauce. Simmer until meat balls are cooked through.
3. Cook macaroni according to directions on packages; drain.
4. Arrange on individual plates with 2 meat balls. Cover with sauce and serve with Parmesan cheese.

Serves 50.

CHEESE AND MACARONI

5 pounds elbow macaroni
1 pound butter or margarine
2 cups sifted flour
¼ cup salt
2 teaspoons pepper

6 tablespoons dry mustard
4 quarts milk
6 pounds grated American cheese
3 cups buttered breadcrumbs*

1. Preheat the oven to 350 degrees.
2. Boil macaroni according to directions on package until tender. Drain and rinse with cold water.
3. Melt butter or margarine in a large saucepan.
4. Stir flour, salt, pepper and dry mustard into butter or margarine. Add milk slowly, stirring constantly until thickened.
5. Add American cheese. Stir until well blended. Combine cheese sauce with macaroni and pour into 2 baking pans (11″ × 16″ × 2½″). Sprinkle breadcrumbs on mixture. Bake 30 minutes.

Serves 50.

*Buttered Breadcrumbs: Mix 3 cups fine dry breadcrumbs with ¾ cup butter or margarine, melted.

NOODLE-CORN CASSEROLE

2 tablespoons shortening
1 pound ground beef
1 medium onion, sliced very thin
1½ teaspoons salt
Dash of pepper
1 teaspoon Worcestershire sauce

1 (8 ounce) can condensed cream of
  celery soup
1 soup can water
1 (1 pound) can cream-style corn
2 cups (4 ounces) fine noodles
Chopped parsley

1. Heat shortening in skillet and brown beef, discarding fat.
2. Combine all ingredients except noodles and parsley in slow cooker.
3. Cook on high 3 hours.
4. Add noodles and cook until done (about 15 minutes.) Serve with chopped parsley.
Makes 4 servings.

SALMON MACARONI SALAD

4 pounds Ditalini
8 (1 pound) cans red salmon
16 medium tomatoes
1 medium onion chopped
3 quarts thinly sliced celery

8 medium diced cucumbers
8 medium diced green peppers
4 tablespoons salt
2 quarts mayonnaise

1. Boil Ditalini in salted water until tender. Drain and blanch with cold water to chill; drain again. Place in large bowl.
2. Remove salmon skin and bones and flake. Cut tomatoes in wedges.
3. Add onion, celery, cucumbers, green peppers, salt and mayonnaise to macaroni and mix all together lightly with 2 forks. Garnish with stuffed olives, hard boiled eggs and radish roses if desired.
Serves 50.

CHICKEN TETRAZZINI

3 cups diced cooked chicken
2 cups chicken stock
½ cup finely chopped onion
½ cup white wine
½ pound sliced mushrooms

1 (8 ounce) can condensed cream of
   mushroom soup
8 ounces spaghetti
Grated Parmesan cheese

1. Combine all ingredients except spaghetti and cheese in slow cooker. Stir well.
2. Cook on high 1 hour, then switch to low 6–8 hours. Or cook on automatic 7 hours.
3. Cook spaghetti according to directions on package; drain and serve with sauce and sprinkle with cheese.

Makes 5–6 servings.

MINESTRONE

½ cup diced salt pork
¼ pound ham, minced
1 (1-pound) can chickpeas
½ cup minced onion
1 clove minced garlic
½ cup diced carrots
½ cup diced celery

1 cup fresh chopped spinach
1 fresh tomato diced
1 medium diced potato
2 tablespoons chopped parsley
1 quart chicken broth
½ cup elbow macaroni
Grated Parmesan cheese

1. Sauté salt pork and discard fat.
2. Combine all ingredients except macaroni and cheese in slow cooker. Add water if chicken broth does not cover.
3. Cook on high 1 hour, then switch to low 6–8 hours. Or cook on automatic 5–6 hours.
4. One half hour before serving, add macaroni. Serve soup generously sprinkled with cheese.

Makes 6 servings.

SPINACH CASSEROLE

2 cups medium noodles
2 packages frozen chopped spinach,
    thawed
½ cup chopped onion
1 cup grated Cheddar or Swiss cheese

¼ cup butter or margarine
Dash of nutmeg
1 can condensed cream of
    mushroom soup

1. Cook noodles until just slightly tender; drain.
2. Combine all remaining ingredients in slow cooker.
3. Cook on high 1 hour, then switch to low 4–5 hours. Or cook on automatic 3–4 hours.
Makes 8 servings.

SPAGHETTI SAUCE

2 tablespoons shortening
2 pounds ground beef
1 cup chopped onion
1 cup chopped green pepper
2 cloves crushed garlic
1 cup chopped mushrooms

2 (28 ounce) cans tomatoes
1 (6 ounce) can tomato paste
2 teaspoons salt
3 teaspoons oregano
½ teaspoon rosemary
¼ teaspoon thyme

1. Heat shortening in skillet and brown beef, discarding fat.
2. Combine all ingredients in slow cooker, stirring well.
3. Cook on low 10–12 hours, on high 5–6 hours, or on automatic 6 hours.
Makes 2 quarts sauce.

MACARONI-SHRIMP CURRY

1 pound cooked, cleaned shrimp, cut into
    pieces if desired
1 cup chopped onions
½ cup sliced celery
1 cup chopped apple
½ cup shredded coconut
½ cup chopped walnuts
1 teaspoon salt

¼ teaspoon pepper
1 tablespoon curry powder
¼ teaspoon ginger
2 (8 ounce) cans condensed cream of
    celery soup
½ cup water
1 (8 ounce) package elbow macaroni

1. Combine all ingredients except macaroni in slow cooker and stir.
2. Cook on low 6–8 hours, or on high 4 hours.
3. Cook macaroni according to directions on package; drain. Add macaroni to curry and heat.

Serves 6.

Note: May be doubled for 6 quart cooker.

126

PASTA COOKING GUIDE FOR MICROWAVE COOKERY

For Pastas, fill a 3-quart container ¾ full of water. Heat in microwave oven 6 to 8 minutes. Then add Pasta and cook according to the following chart.

Kind	Amount	Heat	Stand
Cannelloni* Lasagne* Linguini* Macaroni* Noodles* Shells, Small* Spaghetti*	7 to 8 oz.	7–10 min. uncovered	Drain, rinse and let stand 3–4 min., uncovered
Manicotti** Shells, Jumbo**	8 to 10 oz.	9–12 min. uncovered	Drain, rinse and let stand 3–4 min., covered
Spaghetti* Elbow or Rings* Vermicelli*	10 to 12 oz.		Standing time is unnecessary when Pasta is to be used in casserole

* Add 1 teaspoon salt
**Add 1½ teaspoons salt

MICROWAVE OVEN SPAGHETTI SAUCE

2 pounds ground pork and beef or all beef
¼ cup olive oil
1 cup fresh chopped mushrooms
1 medium chopped onion
1 chopped green pepper
1 minced clove garlic
1 teaspoon mustard

1 tablespoon sugar
1 teaspoon oregano
1 (28-ounce) can tomatoes
1 (15-ounce) can tomato sauce
2 (6 ounce) cans tomato paste
2 tablespoons Worcestershire sauce

1. Heat browning dish in microwave oven 4 minutes. Brown meat in olive oil in it 7–8 minutes.
2. Add mushrooms, onion, peppers and garlic and heat 4 minutes.
3. Stir in mustard, sugar, oregano, tomatoes, tomato sauce, tomato paste and Worcestershire sauce. Heat 4 minutes. Makes 2 quarts. Serve with Pasta cooked according to chart (p. 127).

Microwave time: 15 minutes.

FRUIT-NOODLE KUGEL

2 quarts water
1 (8 ounce) package broad noodles
1 teaspoon salt
3 beaten eggs
¼ cup sugar
1 teaspoon cinnamon
¼ cup melted salted butter
1 teaspoon vanilla

1 cup sour cream
¼ cup milk
1 pound creamed cottage cheese
1 (8 ounce) can drained fruit cocktail
½ cup cornflakes
½ teaspoon cinnamon
3 teaspoons butter
½ teaspoon cinnamon

1. Heat water in a large 3 quart casserole in microwave oven for 3 minutes. Place noodles and salt in hot water in microwave oven and heat 4 minutes. Drain water from noodles.
2. Mix eggs, sugar, cinnamon, butter, vanilla, sour cream, milk, cottage cheese, and fruit cocktail together and then blend with cooked noodles. Set in microwave oven and heat 12 minutes.
3. Mix cornflakes and cinnamon. Top casserole with this mixture and dot with butter. Continue to heat 3–5 minutes more.

Serves 6–8. Microwave time: 25–28 minutes.

WHEAT AND NOODLE PILAF (Bulghour and Noodles)

2 tablespoons butter
2 handfuls small egg noodles

1 cup cracked wheat, coarse grained
1½ cups chicken or meat broth

1. Heat browning dish in microwave oven 4 minutes. Melt butter in it and brown the noodles; heat 1–3 minutes, stirring often.
2. Add wheat and broth and cover; heat 5 minutes.

Serves 4–6.

Microwave time: 10–12 minutes.

An unusual noodle accompaniment with most entrées.

LA ROSA FAMILY

PASTA

FAVORITES

    While four generations of La Rosa men have been preparing highest quality macaroni products, their wives have been perfecting family pasta recipes which, until now, have been passed down from generation to generation within the family. For the first time, La Rosa women are sharing them with you.

LA ROSA FAMILY STUFFED MANICOTTI

Sauce

1 clove garlic
1 medium minced onion
6 tablespoons olive oil
2 (16-ounce) cans tomatoes
1 (16-ounce) can tomato sauce

2 tablespoons chopped parsley
1 teaspoon salt
½ teaspoon basil
Dash of pepper
1 teaspoon sugar

Cheese Filling

1 pound Ricotta or cottage cheese
¼ pound Mozzarella cheese,
    finely chopped or grated
1 tablespoon finely chopped parsley

3 tablespoons grated Parmesan cheese
2 teaspoons sugar
1 lightly beaten egg
Salt and pepper to taste

Meat Filling

¼ pound pork sausage
2 tablespoons olive oil
2 tablespoons chopped onion
2 tablespoons chopped green pepper
½ pound ground beef
½ teaspoon salt

2 tablespoons of the above sauce
¼ cup soft breadcrumbs
¼ pound Mozzarella cheese,
    grated or diced
½ tablespoon chopped parsley
Dash of pepper

Manicotti

1 (5 ounce) package Manicotti
Grated Parmesan cheese to taste

1. To make the sauce, sauté garlic and onion in olive oil several minutes. Add tomatoes, tomato sauce and seasonings and simmer, uncovered until thickened, about 20 minutes. Makes 6 cups sauce.
2. For this recipe fill with either the cheese or the meat filling. To make the cheese filling combine all ingredients listed, blending and mixing together well. Fill uncooked Manicotti and bake as directed below.
3. To make the meat filling, crumble the sausage meat and brown lightly in hot oil with onion, green pepper and ground beef. Drain off excess fat and cool. When cooled, combine with remaining ingredients, lightly but thoroughly. If too dry, add a little more sauce. Fill uncooked Manicotti and bake as directed below.
4. Preheat the oven to 350 degrees.
5. Pour a little sauce in the bottom of a baking dish and then fill each Manicotti with a teaspoon of sauce. Arrange side by side in the dish. Cover with sauce and bake, covered with aluminum foil, for 40 minutes. Then cook uncovered for another 5–10 minutes. Sprinkle with grated Parmesan cheese and serve.

Serves 4–6.

NINA'S* SPAGHETTINI WITH GARLIC AND PARSLEY

Nina is the wife of Pasqueale La Rosa, third son of the founder.

½ cup olive oil
4 sliced garlic cloves
1 pound Spaghettini

2 tablespoons chopped parsley
Grated Parmesan cheese

1. Heat the oil in a large iron skillet, if you can lift it. Otherwise, any heavy skillet will do. Sauté the garlic in the oil for 3 minutes and then discard it. By now the oil should be nice and hot.
2. Meanwhile, cook the Spaghettini according to directions on the package; drain.
3. Pour all the cooked Spaghettini into the pan with the garlic. It will splatter a little, but that is good. Sprinkle all the parsley over the Spaghettini and stir, lifting and turning gently. As soon as all the strands are well coated, slide the Spaghettini into a large platter and sprinkle on a generous helping of Parmesan cheese.

Serves 4–6.

PEGGY LA ROSA'S* SPAGHETTI WITH TRUFFLE SAUCE

Third generation La Rosa family member, Peggy is married to Vincent S. La Rosa, a grandson of the founder.

1 can anchovy fillets
¼ cup olive oil
4 tablespoons butter
3 split garlic cloves
3 tablespoons tomato paste

1¾ cups water
¼ teaspoon freshly ground black pepper
4 or more truffles, cut julienne style
1 pound spaghetti

1. Drain and rinse the anchovies in cold water, then drain again and chop them up in very small pieces.
2. Heat the oil and butter in a heavy saucepan and saute the garlic for about 3 minutes, then discard it. Drop in the anchovies and mix with a wooden spoon. Stir in the tomato paste mixed with water and pepper. Bring the whole mixture to a boil, then simmer over low heat for about 20 minutes. Add the truffles. Taste for seasoning.
3. Meanwhile, cook the spaghetti according to directions on package; drain. Heap the spaghetti into a deep and hot serving dish. Add the sauce and lift and turn the spaghetti quickly and lightly until all the strands are coated.

Serves 4–6.

Note: This is an elegant dish for an elegant dinner party.

KATHLEEN LA ROSA'S*
SPAGHETTINI WITH MUSHROOMS AND ANCHOVIES

Third generation La Rosa family member, Kathleen is married to Vincent F. La Rosa, a grandson of the founder.

¼ cup olive oil
6 anchovy fillets, finely chopped
2 cloves garlic, minced
¼ pound sliced fresh mushrooms
¾ cup dry white wine

Dash dried crushed red peppers
1 pound tomatoes, peeled and chopped
1 pound Spaghettini
3 tablespoons minced parsley

1. Heat the oil in a skillet. Sauté the anchovies and garlic for 2 minutes. Add the mushrooms and cook for another 2 minutes. Mix in the wine. Cook for 2 minutes over very high heat. Add the peppers and tomatoes, and cook for 20 minutes over low heat. Taste for seasoning.
2. Meanwhile, cook the Spaghettini according to package directions. Pour the sauce over the Spaghettini and sprinkle with the parsley. Serve immediately.

Serves 4–6.

ROSE LA ROSA'S*
WHITE CLAM SAUCE WITH SPAGHETTI

Third generation La Rosa family member, Rose is married to Joseph S. La Rosa, a grandon of the founder.

2 quarts tiny hard-shelled clams
½ cup olive oil
¾ cup finely chopped onions
2 cloves minced garlic

¼ teapoon freshly ground black pepper
⅓ cup minced parsley
1 pound spaghetti

1. Scrub the clams thoroughly with a brush, and rinse them under running water until the water runs clean. Place in a saucepan and cover. Cook over high heat until shells open. Shake the pan frequently while on the stove. Remove the clams from the shells and strain the juice. If any of the shells haven't opened, just toss them out.
2. In another suacepan, heat the oil. Add the onions and sauté 5 minutes. Toss in garlic and sauté another 5 minutes. Add the steamed clams, juice, pepper and parsley. Cook one minute.
3. Meanwhile, cook the spaghetti according to package instructions; drain. Spoon the clam sauce over the spaghetti. Hurry and eat!

Serves 4–6.

MARGARET LA ROSA'S*
SAUCE WITH DIFFERENT KINDS OF SPICY MEATBALLS

Third generation La Rosa family member, Margaret is married to Phillip La Rosa, a grandson of the founder.

1 pound lean chopped beef
½ cup finely chopped onions
½ cup soft breadcrumbs
3 tablespoons ketchup
2 lightly beaten eggs
Dash of salt
Dash of pepper
¼ teaspoon cinnamon
¼ teaspoon ground cloves

¼ teaspoon nutmeg
Maybe bacon, walnuts or something else
2 tablespoons olive oil
1 (8 ounce) can tomato sauce
1 cup water
1 cup chopped celery
1 pound thin spaghetti
½ cup grated Parmesan cheese

1. In a large bowl mix the beef, onions, breadcrumbs, ketchup, egg, salt and pepper. Divide the mixture into four portions. In the first portion, mix the cinnamon. In the second, the cloves. In the third nutmeg. In the fourth . . . improvise. (You might like to try bacon, walnuts, or whatever your imagination can come up with.) Shape each of the portions into balls of different size (clove portion, ½ inch balls, cinnamon 1 inch, etc).
2. Heat the oil in a saucepan, and brown the meatballs. Add the tomato sauce, water and celery. Cook over low heat for about 15 minutes.
3. Cook the spaghetti according to package directions; drain. Pour the meatballs and sauce over the spaghetti, and sprinkle with grated Parmesan cheese.
Serves 4–6.

GRANDMA LA ROSA'S*
FAMOUS CHICKEN STUFFED WITH MACARONI

Grandma La Rosa was the wife of the founder, Vincenzo La Rosa.

1 (4 pound) chicken
6 cups water
1 stalk celery with leaves
1 small onion
2½ teaspoons salt
4 tablespoons butter
3 tablespoons flour

½ cup light cream
¼ teaspoon freshly ground black pepper
Dash of nutmeg
½ pound shell macaroni
1 cup sliced and sautéed fresh mushrooms
½ cup grated Parmesan cheese

1. Clean and wash the chicken. Place in a deep saucepan with the water, celery, onion and 2 teaspoons salt. Bring to a boil. Cover and cook over low heat 1½ hours, or until the chicken is tender. Drain the chicken and keep hot. Strain and reserve 1 cup of chicken stock.
2. Preheat oven to 400 degrees.
3. Melt the butter in a saucepan, and blend in the flour. Add the 1 cup reserved stock and cream, stirring constantly. When the sauce begins to boil, add the pepper, nutmeg, and remaining ½ teaspoon salt. Cook over low heat for 5 minutes.
4. Cook the macaroni according to directions on package; drain. Toss the macaroni with half the sauce and the mushrooms. Stuff the chicken with the mixture and close the opening. Place breast side up in a well-buttered baking pan. Pour the remaining sauce on top. Bake for 10 minutes. Sprinkle with the cheese and bake 5 minutes longer or until the cheese is delicately browned.

Serves 4–6.

VITA LA ROSA'S*
LASAGNE WITH HOT AND SWEET SAUSAGES

Vita is the wife of Stefano La Rosa, second son of the founder.

¼ pound Italian hot sausage
¼ pound Italian sweet sausage
1 small onion
6 tablespoons butter
¾ cup dry white wine
1 tablespoon tomato paste

1 tablespoon hot water
1 pound Lasagne
1 pound Mozzarella cheese
2 pounds Ricotta or cottage cheese
1 cup grated Parmesan cheese

1. Preheat the oven to 320 degrees.
2. Prick the hot and sweet sausages, and boil them in water for 4 minutes. Drain off fat, peel and chop. Reserve.
3. Mince onion and sauté in 2 tablespoons of the butter until soft and golden. Then add the chopped sausage and sauté for 5 minutes. Add white wine and simmer until almost evaporated. Thin the tomato paste with hot water and stir into the sauce. Cover and simmer gently for 10 to 15 minutes. Thin again with boiling water if needed.
4. Cook Lasagne according to directions on package; drain. Butter a 3-quart baking dish and put into it a layer of Lasagne. Spoon over some of the sauce, cover with a layer of sliced Mozzarella and another layer of Lasagne. Spoon over more sauce and a layer of Ricotta or cottage cheese. Then another layer of Lasagne. Repeat until sauce, cheese and Lasagne are all used up. End with a layer of Lasagne. Sprinkle with grated Parmesan cheese and dot with bits of remaining butter.
5. Bake until it puffs and bubbles (half an hour or so.)

Serves 4–6.

MILLIE LA ROSA'S* QUICKIE MACARONI AND BEEF CASSEROLE

Millie is the wife of Peter La Rosa, fifth son of the founder.

¼ cup chopped onions
¼ cup chopped green peppers
3 tablespoons butter
1 pound ground beef
½ teaspoon salt

¼ teaspoon freshly ground pepper
2 tablespoons paprika
1 (15½ ounce) jar prepared meat sauce
1 package elbow macaroni

1. Using a heavy skillet on an even heat, sauté onions and green peppers in butter for 5 minutes.
2. Add the ground beef and, crumbling it with a fork, cook until browned. Stir constantly. Sprinkle with salt, pepper, and paprika. Stir in meat sauce; blend well, heating thoroughly.
3. Cook elbow macaroni according to directions on package; drain. Cook in the meat and sauce mixture for 5 minutes. Taste for seasoning and serve.

Serves 4–6.

JOSEPHINE LA ROSA'S* SAUCE WITH WINE

Josephine La Rosa, a granddaughter of the founder.

2 tablespoons olive oil
1 pound ground beef
¾ cup chopped onions
1 clove minced garlic
2 cups wine
1 (28 ounce) can tomatoes
1 (6 ounce) can tomato paste

2 bay leaves
1 teaspoon basil
a big bunch of oregano
1½ teaspoons salt
2 tablespoons chopped parsley
2 tablespoons melted butter
1 pound spaghetti

1. Heat the olive oil in a saucepan. Mix in the beef, onions and garlic. Cook over high heat, stirring constantly until the meat is browned. Add one cup of the wine, and cook for another 2 minutes over high heat or until the wine is almost evaporated. Add the tomatoes, tomato paste, bay leaves, basil, oregano and salt. Cover and cook over low heat for ½ hour. Add the second cup of wine, and cook for another hour. Stir in the parsley and melted butter and extract the bay leaves.
2. Cook the spaghetti according to package instructions; drain. Pour the sauce over the spaghetti and serve immediately.

Serves 4–6.

MARY LA ROSA'S* FETTUCCINE WITH HAM AND EGGS

Mary La Rosa is the wife of Filippo La Rosa, fourth son of the founder.

¼ pound butter
½ cup chopped onion
¼ pound cooked ham
½ cup sliced and sautéed mushrooms

4 egg yolks
4 tablespoons freshly grated
  Parmesan cheese
1 pound Fettuccine

1. Melt 2 tablespoons butter in a skillet. Sauté the onions and ham for 5 minutes. Stir in the sautéed mushrooms, and season to taste.
2. Beat the egg yolks in the top of a double boiler. Stir in the cheese and the rest of the butter, cut in small pieces. Place over hot water, and stir constantly with a wooden spoon until thickened. Make sure the water does not boil.
3. Meanwhile, cook the Fettuccine according to package instructions; drain. Put the drained Fettuccine in a hot bowl; pour the egg mixture over it and toss very well. Sprinkle the ham mixture on top.

Serves 4–6.

RECIPE INDEX

143